Everyday Life:
RENAISSANCE

WALTER A. HAZEN

A GOOD YEAR BOOK™

GOOD YEAR BOOKS
Tucson, Arizona

Dedication

To Martha, Jordan, and Allison.

Acknowledgments

Grateful acknowledgment is extended to Roberta Dempsey, Editorial Director at Good Year Books, who patiently guided me through this addition to the "Everyday Life series. Without her advice and support, this book would not have been possible.

I would also like to thank Helen Fisher, Publisher at Good Year Books for giving me the opportunity to continue the "Everyday Life" series. Her support and confidence in me is likewise appreciated.

Good Year Books

are available for most basic curriculum subjects plus many enrichment areas. For more Good Year Books, contact your local bookseller or educational dealer. For a complete catalog with information about other Good Year Books, please contact:

Good Year Books
P. O. Box 91858
Tucson, Arizona 85752
1-800-511-1530
www.goodyearbooks.com

Editor: Roberta Dempsey
Cover Design: Ronan Design
Interior Design: Dan Miedaner

Table of Contents

Introduction	**1**
Chapter 1—**The Background**	**2**
Fill in a Map of Italy	6
Distinguish between Fact and Opinion	7
Make False Statements True	8
Use Your Critical-Thinking Skills	9
Chapter 2—**New Ways of Thinking**	**10**
Solve a Humanism Puzzle	14
Point Out the Differences	15
Name Those Synonyms and Antonyms	16
Keep a Time-Traveler Diary	17
Chapter 3—**Two Great Artists**	**18**
Solve Some Sistine Chapel Math	22
Use Context Clues to Complete Sentences	23
Write a Lead Paragraph for *The Rome Review*	24
Make a Sketch	25
Chapter 4—**Marriage and Home Life**	**26**
Use Your Critical Thinking Skills	30
Fill in a Venn Diagram	31
Solve Wedding-Related Math	32
Complete a Word Search	33
Chapter 5—**Fashion and Food**	**34**
Sketch a Costume	38
Match Foods and Countries	39
Write a Blurb for a Book on Clothing	40
Solve a Fashion and Food Puzzle	41
Chapter 6—**Fun and Amusements**	**42**
Interpret a Pie Graph	46
Conduct a Survey	47
Indicate Which Word Does Not Belong	48
Make a Shoe-Box Diorama	49

Table of Contents *continued*

Chapter 7— **Manners and Behavior**   **50**
Think about Etiquette   54
Complete a Checklist   55
Point Out the Good and the Bad   56
Write a Letter to the Editor   57

Chapter 8— **Scientific Discoveries**   **58**
Rank the Discoveries   62
Research the Solar System   63
Make False Statements True   64
Create a Dialogue   65

Chapter 9— **Exploration and Discovery**   **66**
Name That Notable   70
Make a Cereal-Box Report   71
Use Your Critical Thinking Skills   72
Solve Some Exploration Math   73

Chapter 10— **Great Religious Changes**   **74**
Conduct an Interview   78
Solve a Protestant Revolt Puzzle   79
Organize Organized Religion   80
Complete a Chain of Events Staircase   81

Chapter 11— **The Renaissance Spreads**   **82**
Write Your Opinions   86
Make a Drawing of the Globe Theater   87
Distinguish between Sentences and Fragments   88
Write a Summary   89

Answers to Activities   **90**

Additional Resources   **92**

From *Everyday Life: The Renaissance* © 2005 Good Year Books.

Introduction

Upon seeing a book with the word *Renaissance* in the title, you probably think of achievements in art, literature, and science. The names of Michelangelo, Leonardo da Vinci, William Shakespeare, and others quickly come to mind. This is the Renaissance with which most people are familiar. The Renaissance was a time when actors, writers, sculptors, inventors, and many other talented individuals flourished. As with every period of history, the Renaissance was also a time of everyday life—a time when people went about their daily routines much as we do today. What these people thought and felt is every bit as important as the contributions they made.

Everyday Life: The Renaissance, introduces students to the achievements of the most talented artists and writers of the day. They are also given a brief survey of important scientific breakthroughs and major explorations that led to the discovery of a New World. The religious upheaval of the 1500s that resulted in the founding of the world's various Protestant churches is also presented. The focus of the book, however, remains the same as with previous *Everyday Life* books. Primary coverage is given to how people thought and behaved, how they dressed and what they ate, what they did for fun and amusement, and how they viewed marriage and home life.

Each chapter of this book is followed by four pages of activities. Some test a student's ability to think creatively; others measure skills in math, vocabulary, and other subject areas. There are also numerous arts-and-crafts activities that provide further insight into the Renaissance way of life. There are even a few puzzles for enjoyment. Students should find *Everyday Life: The Renaissance* engaging and informative.

Walter A. Hazen

CHAPTER 1

The Background

For about 500 years after the fall of the Roman Empire (30 B.C.–A.D. 476) in the West, European civilization passed through a period when little human progress was made. Learning and organized government came to a virtual halt. Historians called this period the *Dark Ages.*

The Dark Ages resulted from barbarian invasions into lands once ruled by Rome. The German tribes that overran Rome had little respect for either culture or law and order. They destroyed magnificent buildings and precious works of art. Roads that united the vast expanses of the Empire fell into disrepair, and trade declined as a result. With no central authority to keep order, travel became dangerous. People were afraid to venture outside their own villages or towns. Society as the Romans knew it ceased to exist.

A Viking ship under sail.

One German king, Charlemagne, temporarily restored law and order over much of Europe in the late 700s and early 800s. The empire he founded did not endure, however. After its breakup, invaders swept across Europe. Beginning in the 800s, the Vikings stormed out of Scandinavia, and chaos prevailed once more. The Vikings were fierce warriors who struck terror in the hearts of people everywhere. They came from what are now the countries of Norway, Sweden, and Denmark. Raiding and killing at will, the invaders forced peasants in the countryside to enter into agreements with powerful lords for protection.

For the guarantee of safety inside the walls of a lord's castle or manor house during dangerous times, peasants willingly became serfs. This meant that they were bound to the soil and were a part of the lord's land. They were property; no different from the buildings and fields that made up a manor. If a manor was sold, the serfs were handed over to the new owner as part of the sale. The arrangement between serf and lord, along with agreements reached between lords and knights, became the basis of the feudal system.

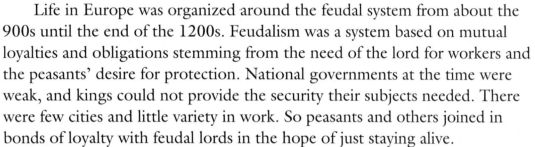

Life in Europe was organized around the feudal system from about the 900s until the end of the 1200s. Feudalism was a system based on mutual loyalties and obligations stemming from the need of the lord for workers and the peasants' desire for protection. National governments at the time were weak, and kings could not provide the security their subjects needed. There were few cities and little variety in work. So peasants and others joined in bonds of loyalty with feudal lords in the hope of just staying alive.

Little changed until the time of the Crusades (1095–1291). These were military expeditions to recapture the Holy Land (Palestine) from the Muslim Turks. Although the place where Jesus lived was never permanently taken, the Crusaders saw and learned things that influenced Europe forever. For the first time, European lords and ordinary soldiers and pilgrims marveled at great cities and at the culture and learning of the Greek and Arab worlds. They brought back unusual foods, such as sugar, spices, and rice, and told friends of such luxuries as silks, rugs, precious stones, paper, and glassware. The Crusaders' tales of adventure and discovery made Europeans realize that there was a world and ways of living different than their own.

Crusaders preparing to do battle.

More importantly, the Crusades helped weaken the landed nobility of western Europe and brought about the decline of feudalism. Although some elements of the feudal system survived for several more centuries, the age of independent feudal lords, serfs, and knights came to an end. Without such an occurrence, the Renaissance could not have taken place. As long as life centered around the castle and the manor house, and travel and trade were virtually nonexistent, little progress was made. The Crusades and their aftermath brought about dramatic changes in the ways people thought about their world. Feudalism gradually weakened.

How, you might ask, did the Crusades weaken feudalism? The answer is simple. Nobles who went on the Crusades needed money. It cost a lot to finance an expedition that might take several years. To raise funds, feudal lords sold charters to towns under their control. These towns later became independent and self-governing. Many who set out for the Holy Land never returned. Untold numbers were killed and others stayed in the lands they visited and carved out new estates for themselves. Their manors back home were broken up and their serfs moved to the towns. The elimination of so many powerful nobles made it possible for kings to expand their control over

wider areas. The growth of central control led to greater security, an increase in trade, the growth of towns, and a revival of learning. These factors in turn led to the Renaissance.

Another factor that weakened feudalism was the introduction of new weapons. Until the Crusades began in the 1000s, the medieval knight in his suit of armor was nearly invincible. About the only way to get the better of a knight was to knock him off his horse and stab him in an unprotected part of his body, at the neck. This was considered a complete violation of the rules of war.

Then came the longbow. First used by the English against the French at the battle of Crécy in 1346, the longbow was a fearsome weapon. It measured six feet in length and shot a yard-long arrow a distance of between 200 and 400 yards. The force of an arrow propelled from a longbow could pierce a knight's armor. It could also put a knight's horse out of commission, leaving the knight stranded and at the mercy of his enemy. Whereas the more familiar crossbow could fire off one arrow a minute, a longbowman could discharge from five to six a minute. A knight in armor was no match for a foot soldier armed with a longbow. At Crécy, 14,000 English archers and men-at-arms defeated a French force of 20,000 with the aid of the longbow.

What the longbow did for making armored knights obsolete, gunpowder did for castles and walled cities. The Crusaders who went to the Holy Land were introduced to gunpowder by the Muslims, who may have learned about it from the Arabs. The Crusaders also saw guns for the first time. What they saw and learned about weapons in the Middle East changed warfare in Europe forever.

Roger Bacon, an English monk, had published a book about how to make gunpowder as early as 1242. Bacon never actually made the newly-discovered explosive, however. Gunpowder, in fact, did not appear in battle until nearly a century later, when it was used in "firepots." Firepots were early forms of cannon consisting of buckets filled with powder and stones and ignited through a hole in the bottom. As one would suspect, such devices were not very accurate. By the middle of the 1300s, firepots gave way to cannon with tubular barrels that could hurl cannonballs with deadly accuracy against the walls of a castle or fortified city. With his castle's defenses in ruins and his armored knights rendered helpless by superior weapons, the medieval feudal lord quickly went the way of the dinosaur.

One other factor helped end feudalism and make the Renaissance possible. That was the terrible Black Death that raged through western Europe in 1351.

From *Everyday Life: The Renaissance* © 2005 Good Year Books.

The Black Death, a form of bubonic plague, had entered Europe through Italy by way of Constantinople, the capital of the Byzantine Empire. It was a contagious disease carried by the fleas of rats. Black splotches appeared on the skin of anyone who contracted the plague, and death came quickly, often within hours.

The number of deaths caused by the plague weakened the power of feudal lords. Some historians maintain that 60,000,000 people, or roughly a third of the population of Europe, died. Many of those who perished were nobles. The majority, however, were common people, all of which made for a shortage of labor on large estates. To bring in their crops, landowners were forced to pay wages to peasants who had previously been serfs. They sometimes also had to rent part of their land to make ends meet. In this way, a disaster unparalleled in European history helped end a system that had held back progress for centuries.

Even though the Black Death had entered Europe through Italy, it was in the Italian city-states that the Renaissance began. There were several reasons why an intellectual revival was born in Italy. First, Italy had been the center of ancient Roman civilization. Many ancient buildings and other reminders of the glory of Rome still existed to inspire, encourage, and motivate both artists and their patrons. Second, feudalism had never been as strong in Italy as in other parts of Europe. Life there was more urban than rural, and many Italian cities had been independent for years. Chief among the Italian city-states were Florence, Genoa, Venice, and Milan.

A final reason why the Renaissance began in Italy had to do with location. Situated on or near the Mediterranean or Adriatic seas, Italian cities had long maintained contact with the advanced civilizations of both the Byzantine Empire (another name for the Eastern Roman Empire) and Muslim-controlled areas all during the Middle Ages. While the rest of Europe existed under the grip of feudalism, Italian cities of Florence, Genoa, Venice, and Milan grew rich from business and trade. It was this wealth flowing into Italian cities that provided the funds to encourage artists, sculptors, and others to create the wondrous works of art we associate with the Renaissance. When trade and business revived in northern and western Europe, this same revival of interest in the arts and learning occurred, and the Renaissance was in full swing.

A woodcut depicts the devil Death taking a child from his family during the Black Death of the fourteenth century.

Name _____ Date _____

Fill in a Map of Italy

Italy did not become a unified nation until 1870. Until that date, it was a country separated into numerous states. During the Middle Ages, even before these states were created, Italy was a land of independent city-states, much in the manner of ancient Greece. A city-state consisted of a large city and its surrounding area. Leading Italian city-states included Florence, Naples, Venice, Milan, Genoa, and Rome.

On the map below, label the cities opposite, as well as the following geographical features: Alps, Apennines, Adriatic Sea, Mediterranean Sea, Po River, Tiber River, Sicily, and Sardinia. Create symbols for cities, mountains, and other important features. Color your map for effect.

From *Everyday Life: The Renaissance* © 2005 Good Year Books.

Name _____ Date _____

Distinguish between Fact and Opinion

A fact is a statement that can be proven. An opinion is only a strong, personal belief. Can you tell the difference between the two?

On the blank line before each of the following sentences, indicate if it is a fact or an opinion by writing "F" or "O."

_____ 1. The feudal system was the way life was organized in Europe during the Middle Ages.

_____ 2. The German tribes that overran the Roman Empire cared little for education and culture.

_____ 3. Charlemagne was one of the greatest kings who ever lived.

_____ 4. The Vikings came from the Scandinavian countries.

_____ 5. The Vikings were no more fierce than other invaders of the time.

_____ 6. Feudalism developed out of a need for protection.

_____ 7. The Muslim rulers of the Middle East were intellectually superior to the Christian Crusaders they fought.

_____ 8. Medieval serfs were satisfied with their life under feudalism.

_____ 9. A foot soldier armed with a longbow had a decided advantage over an armored knight on horseback.

_____ 10. Feudalism in Europe would have lasted centuries longer had it not been for the introduction of gunpowder.

_____ 11. The Renaissance began in Italy because the Italian people were more advanced than Europeans elsewhere.

_____ 12. The Black Death of the 1300s played a role in the decline of feudalism.

_____ 13. Feudalism was never as firmly established in medieval Italy as in other parts of Europe.

_____ 14. Gunpowder was the most important invention of the Middle Ages.

Name _____ Date _____

Make False Statements True

All of the statements on this page are false. Change the word(s) in *italics* to make them true. Write the replacement word(s) on the lines following the statements.

1. The 500-year period following the fall of the Roman Empire is called the *Renaissance*. _____

2. The *Muslims* swept out of Scandinavia in the 800s and terrorized parts of Europe. _____

3. Charlemagne was a *Viking ruler* who temporarily restored order in western Europe in the 800s.

   _____

4. *Strong* national governments were characteristic of the feudal age. _____

5. The Crusades were wars fought to *restore the Roman Empire*. _____

6. The *crossbow* was a weapon capable of piercing a knight's armor. _____

7. Roger Bacon was an English *feudal lord*. _____

8. The Muslims learned about gunpowder from the *Greeks*.

   _____

9. A firepot was an early kind of *stove*. _____

10. The *French* were the first to use the longbow in battle.

    _____

11. The Black Death, or bubonic plague, was a disease spread by people *drinking polluted water*.

    _____

12. Roughly *one-half* of the population of Europe in the 1300s died of the plague. _____

13. The Renaissance began in *France*. _____

14. Italy is a boot-shaped peninsula that juts into the *Baltic* Sea. _____

From *Everyday Life: The Renaissance* © 2005 Good Year Books.

Name _____ Date _____

Use Your Critical-Thinking Skills

Think about the five questions presented here. Then write your best answers to each on the lines provided.

1. What made the Dark Ages "dark" in historical terms?

   _____

   _____

   _____

2. Read the description of a serf in paragraph four of chapter 1. How did a serf differ from a slave?

   _____

   _____

   _____

3. How did the Crusades help bring about the Renaissance?

   _____

   _____

   _____

   _____

4. Why do you think such a large portion of Europe's population succumbed to the Black Death? Think of as many reasons as you can why the death rate was so high.

   _____

   _____

   _____

   _____

5. Why do historians call the Renaissance a bridge between the Middle Ages and modern times?

   _____

   _____

   _____

   _____

New Ways of Thinking

Imagine it is the year 1235. Through a time machine, you have been whisked back to a manor in medieval France. After wandering around for some time, you come upon a serf working in a field. His name is Antoine. He is bent over his plow and is sweating. He looks as if the burden of the world is on his shoulders as he pushes the plow through the thick, black soil.

Antoine barely acknowledges your presence, even though you are dressed in modern clothes and stand out like a strobe light. He simply grunts when you introduce yourself and continues with his work. At length you ask him about his life on the manor and his prospects for the future. He stops for a moment, stares at you as though you've lost your mind, and speaks.

"Prospects for the future? Ha!" he hisses. "I have no prospects for the future. I will live and die on this manor and never venture more than five miles distant. I will work myself to the bone from sunrise to sunset six days a week and probably die before my thirtieth birthday. But it is just as well. The priest tells me I am a worthless sinner, and that my only hope is for a better life in heaven. He also says that the end of the world is near and that my suffering will soon end. So I labor on and live for that day. Life is so hard and miserable, you know."

Peasants at work on a manor.

Troubled by Antoine's pessimism, you re-enter your time machine and set the date 100 years ahead to 1335. This time you are spirited to Florence, in what is now the nation of Italy. You find the contrast hard to believe. You see people going about smiling and chatting away as though they don't have a care in the world. They are obviously happy and show none of the hopelessness displayed by Antoine.

"Why are people now so different from those 100 years ago?" you ask a man who identifies himself as Paolo. "Has everyone gotten away from religion?"

"Not at all," replies Paolo. "We still go to church and follow our religious beliefs, but our thoughts are not focused solely on the hereafter. We believe in the worth of the individual and in his or her right to enjoy life. We believe that people can be happy and live life to the fullest within the framework of religion. We are not obsessed with the doom and gloom of our forebears."

As you are transported back to modern times, you understand completely what Paolo was referring to. He was talking about a new outlook on life called *humanism* and its followers, known as humanists. Humanists were more interested in this life than in the hereafter. They stressed the importance of the individual and praised individual achievements. The humanist outlook was expressed in the words of Leon Battista Alberti, who said, "Men can do all things if they will." Humanists also were more open-minded and more critical than the people of the Middle Ages. They welcomed new ideas and poked fun at superstition and prejudice. They were very critical of the wrongdoings associated with many of the Church clergy at the time. (These wrong-doings are discussed in detail in chapter 11.)

The "Father of Humanism" was an Italian poet and scholar named Francesco Petrarch (1304–1374). He is known simply as Petrarch. Some historians refer to him as "the first modern man." Petrarch was responsible for reviving interest in the forgotten writings of the ancient Greeks and Romans. He and others searched through cellars, musty libraries, and monasteries for old manuscripts that had been painstakingly hand-copied by the monks of the Middle Ages. Sometimes they were successful in their search; at other times they arrived too late to rescue priceless pages. Giovanni Boccaccio (1313–1375), Petrarch's friend and fellow author, wrote how he wept when he once came upon a collection of writings in a monastery that were too deteriorated to salvage.

Petrarch, known in history as the "Father of Humanism."

Why were Petrarch and his associates interested in the literature of civilizations long past? What did the words of the Greeks and Romans hold for people who were beginning to see themselves as modern in every sense? Petrarch believed that people could learn much and find guidance for their lives if they read the classics of such ancient writers as Cicero and Virgil. He saw the Greeks and Romans as having set a standard for daily living that was worthy of imitation. In his enthusiasm, Petrarch not only read Cicero and Virgil, but he wrote imaginary dialogues between each of them and himself.

From *Everyday Life: The Renaissance* © 2005 Good Year Books.

In addition to his encouraging people to study the ancient classics, Petrarch established a pattern of poetry that remained popular throughout the Renaissance period. He did this through a series of sonnets written to a woman he loved from a distance. The lady's name was Laura de Sade, the wife of another man and the mother of 11 children. The fact that she was unavailable did not prevent Petrarch from composing love poems to her. When Laura died of the plague, Petrarch wrote a love poem to her that is considered one of the greatest pieces of poetry ever written.

Humanistic thought reached other parts of Europe through students who had studied at Italian universities. As a result, influential humanists emerged in Germany, France, and other parts of northern and western Europe. Foremost among these was Desiderius Erasmus (1466–1536). Erasmus was a Dutch priest who believed that the Bible could be studied along with the manuscripts of the ancient Greeks and Romans. In his writings, he criticized the ignorance and superstition within the Catholic Church, as well as the wrongdoings of some of the clergy. His aim was to reform the Church and make it better. Unlike a German monk named Martin Luther who lived at the same time and about whom you will read later, Erasmus never gave any thought to breaking away from the Church completely.

Erasmus became so famous in the Netherlands that people applauded him in the street. Common folk sometimes bribed his servants just to peep at him through a keyhole while he slept. Even the candle stubs he threw away were fought over by admiring souvenir hunters. His fame spread elsewhere, and he received offers from universities throughout Europe to serve on their faculties. Many Renaissance writers consider him the greatest scholar of his age.

Nowhere was humanism better exemplified than in art. The contrast between the paintings and sculptures of medieval artists and those of the Renaissance is striking. During the Middle Ages, art focused on religion and was confined to images of the saints and to scenes from the Bible. Scenes in paintings were flat and two-dimensional, and humans portrayed on canvas appeared flat and two-dimensional as well. Artists were viewed more as craftspeople employed by the Church than as individuals creating life-like scenes of the real world. As such, they received no more recognition than carpenters and other artisans.

How different was the art of the Renaissance! Painters and sculptors began to imitate the styles and techniques employed by the Greeks and the Romans. They made the subjects of their paintings and sculptures more real through a

From *Everyday Life: The Renaissance* © 2005 Good Year Books.

variety of techniques. One technique was the use of perspective. This involves painting pictures so as to give them distance and depth.

A good example of using perspective in a picture is the way an artist would paint a railroad track. Had railroads existed in the Middle Ages, the medieval artist would have probably depicted the tracks as having the same width in the distance as in the foreground. The Renaissance artist, on the other hand, would have painted the tracks as though they came together on down the line. Renaissance artists used perspective when painting such objects as buildings and landscapes. The technique created a life-like atmosphere.

Artists also made good use of color, light, and shadows to make people in their pictures more real. Through such devices, they could show feelings and emotions that the medieval artist never attempted. They could even make wrinkles and other skin imperfections stand out on their subjects.

Sculptors also concentrated on making their statues more life-like and natural. In so doing, they leaned heavily on the techniques used by the Greeks and Romans. They

A picture showing how Renaissance artists used perspective to show depth.

sculpted the human body as it really is, with emphasis on natural shape and musculature. In contrast, statues of the Middle Ages appear stiff and unrealistic.

Humanism stressed the importance of the individual in the present world instead of the hereafter. This did not mean, as has previously been mentioned, that Renaissance people abandoned religion in favor of worldly pursuits and pleasures. They simply believed that a person should enjoy life to the fullest during his or her stay on Earth. That, in a nutshell, is what humanism was all about.

Name _____ Date _____

Solve a Humanism Puzzle

Fill in the sentences for clues to complete the puzzle about humanism.

```
_ _ _ H _ _
_ _ U _ _
_ _ M _ _ _
_ _ _ _ A _ _ _
_ _ N _ _ _ _ _ _ _ _
_ _ _ I _ _ _ _
_ _ _ S _ _ _ _ _ _ _
_ _ _ _ M _ _
```

1. Petrarch is known as the _____ of humanism.

2. Petrarch wrote many love poems to _____ de Sade.

3. Humanists admired the works of the ancient Greeks and _____.

4. _____ has been called by some "the first modern man."

5. Humanists searched monasteries and elsewhere for old _____.

6. Medieval art focused mainly on _____.

7. _____ is a technique used by artists to show distance and depth.

8. _____ was a famous Dutch humanist.

From *Everyday Life: The Renaissance* © 2005 Good Year Books.

Name _____ Date _____

Point Out the Differences

On the lines provided, tell how the people of the Renaissance were different from those of the Middle Ages.

Life

_____

_____

_____

_____

_____

_____

_____

_____

_____

Art

_____

_____

_____

_____

_____

_____

_____

_____

Religion

_____

_____

_____

_____

_____

_____

Name _____ Date _____

Name Those Synonyms and Antonyms

A synonym is a word that has the same meaning as another word. An antonym is a word opposite in meaning to another word.

Below is a list of 20 words taken from chapter 2. Write a synonym and an antonym for each. Use a thesaurus or a dictionary, if necessary.

	Synonym	Antonym
1. open-minded (adj)		
2. fame (n)		
3. modern (adj)		
4. worthless (adj)		
5. abandoned (v)		
6. praise (n)		
7. critical (adj)		
8. successful (adj)		
9. arrived (v)		
10. enthusiasm (n)		
11. imaginary (adj)		
12. encouraging (adj)		
13. popular (adj)		
14. continues (v)		
15. applauded (v)		
16. admiring (adj)		
17. rigid (adj)		
18. present (adj)		
19. ignorance (n)		
20. enjoy (v)		

Name _____ Date _____

Keep a Time-Traveler Diary

At the beginning of this chapter, you took an imaginary journey back in time. In the year 1235, you found yourself on a manor in medieval France. One hundred years later, you were in Renaissance Italy marveling at how people's outlook on life had changed.

Create diary entries for each day of these respective years. Record things you might have seen or heard during your brief stopovers.

May 13, 1235

Dear Diary,

_____
_____
_____
_____
_____
_____
_____
_____
_____
_____
_____
_____

April 4, 1335

Dear Diary,

_____
_____
_____
_____
_____
_____
_____
_____
_____
_____
_____
_____

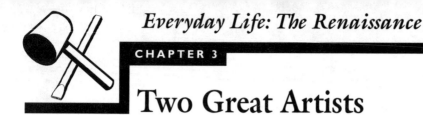
Two Great Artists

The Renaissance produced many great artists. You may have heard of Leonardo da Vinci, Michelangelo, Raphael, Rembrandt, and Holbein, to name a few. There were many others. Because the focus of this book is on everyday life during the time and not on the works of individual artists, only two, Leonardo da Vinci and Michelangelo Buonarroti, will be discussed in some detail. These two are among the more famous.

Leonardo da Vinci's "flying machine," which he envisioned as being operated by a man seated in the middle.

Leonardo da Vinci was born in 1452 in the village of Vinci, in what is now Italy. What little is known of his early life is taken from the diary of his grandfather, Ser Antonio, with whom he lived until he was five years old. Ser Antonio revealed that Leonardo's father was a notary and his mother a peasant girl. His father married several times while Leonardo was a young boy.

From an early age, Leonardo showed an interest in everything around him. He collected flowers, leaves, unusual pieces of wood, and even small animals. He drew pictures of everything he saw on his walks through the countryside. Unlike others his age, he seemed to have an unquenchable thirst for knowledge. This thirst would in time make him one of the most remarkable men of the Renaissance.

At the age of 15, Leonardo was apprenticed to a painter and sculptor in Florence named Andrea Verrocchio. He remained and worked with Verrocchio until 1477, although he had progressed so quickly that he was admitted to the painters' guild as a master in 1472 at the age of 20. Leonardo studied not only painting and sculpture under Verrocchio but engineering as well. By the time he was 25 he had surpassed his tutor in skill and was ready to move on to other endeavors.

After leaving Verrocchio, Leonardo went to work for Lorenzo de Medici, the richest and most powerful man in Florence. Lorenzo paid Leonardo to paint and sculpt. Later, Leonardo worked for the ruler of Milan. Then he

moved on to other patrons, the last being King Francis I of France. Francis I gave Leonardo a chateau, a beautiful country house. He worked in France until his death in 1519.

Leonardo was a "jack-of-all-trades." Above all, he was a magnificent painter and sculptor. He created two of the world's greatest paintings: *Last Supper* and *Mona Lisa*, the latter a portrait of a lady thought to be Lisa del Gioconda. But he was also an architect, scientist, mathematician, engineer, and philosopher. More than 7,000 pages of his notebooks survive, and they reveal a person interested in every aspect of life. Even the notebooks themselves are fascinating. Besides containing notes and sketches of people, plants, animals, and machines, they are composed in "mirror" writing. Leonardo was ambidextrous and could write with either hand. Therefore, to protect his notes from prying eyes, he wrote them backward with his left hand and read them later in a mirror.

The drawings included in Leonardo's notebooks point to his curiosity about everything around him. There are many sketches of the human body that accurately depict muscles and tendons. These he obtained by dissecting the bodies of executed criminals. There are even more drawings of flying machines, submarines, and machine guns. In time, Leonardo's imaginings gave way to reality.

Some people found Leonardo a strange man. He bought caged birds in the marketplace and immediately set them free. Yet he would imprison flies to study the flapping of their wings. He recorded the varied sounds made when he clipped the wings of some and coated the flapping wings of others with honey. He would also spend hours on the banks of a river with his ear pressed against a submerged tube, listening to the sounds made by the moving water.

No person better exemplified the spirit of the Renaissance than Leonardo da Vinci. Nothing escaped his critical eye, as he sought answers to every problem of the day. Yet at the same time, and in true Renaissance fashion, he enjoyed everyday life. He loved a good joke and acquired a reputation as a prankster. Once at a party in Rome he inflated the entrails of a ram with bellows, causing them to rise like balloons and scare the guests in an adjacent room within an inch of their lives. Even in fun, Leonardo upheld the spirit of the age!

Michelangelo Buonarroti may have never been the life of a Renaissance party, but he was in many ways just as versatile as Leonardo da Vinci. Known simply as Michelangelo, he was a gifted painter, sculptor, architect, and amateur

poet. Although some scholars consider his greatest work to be the religious scenes he painted on the ceiling of the Sistine Chapel in the Pope's palace in Rome, Michelangelo thought himself above all a sculptor. His works certainly support his claim. His statues of David and Moses are among the world's greatest sculptures. And few are not moved when they gaze upon the *Pietá,* Michelangelo's sculpture of the dead Jesus in his grieving mother's lap.

Michelangelo's *Pietá, a* magnificent sculpture of the dead Christ on his mother's knees. Carved from a single slab of marble, the *Pietá* stands in Saint Peter's Church in Rome.

That Michelangelo achieved so much in his lifetime is remarkable considering his beginnings. Born in 1475 in a small village and raised in Florence, he was a small and sickly child. His father was a former public official who beat him regularly because of his interest in painting. His uncles ridiculed him, maintaining that art was work suited only for peasants. Surely the son of a public official could find something better to do with his life.

When at last Michelangelo's father realized that his son was determined to become an artist, he apprenticed him to a painter named Domenico Ghirlandaio. Michelangelo was 13 at the time. A year later, he began to study sculpture under Bertoldo de Giovanni, who just happened to be in charge of the personal gardens of Lorenzo de Medici. Lorenzo de Medici, you will remember, was once the patron of Leonardo da Vinci. In a similar manner, this powerful man took Michelangelo under his wing and treated him as his own son.

When Michelangelo was 33, he was commissioned by Pope Julius II to paint scenes from the Bible on the ceiling of the Sistine Chapel. Michelangelo was reluctant at first, telling the pope he was a sculptor, not a painter. But Julius II was insistent, and Michelangelo gave in. He signed a contract for the project in 1508 and set about making his plans.

The Sistine Chapel in the Vatican in Rome is no small place. It measures 132 feet by 45 feet and the ceiling covers some 3,000 square feet. The ceiling is about 70 feet above the floor, which gives you some idea of the difficulty Michelangelo faced when he began his task. All work would have to be done on a high scaffold with Michelangelo flat on his back.

From *Everyday Life: The Renaissance* © 2005 Good Year Books.

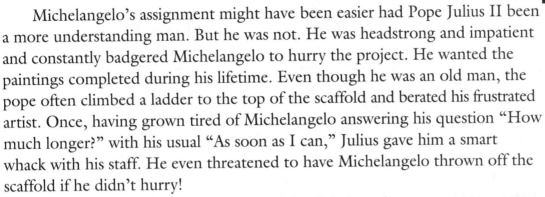

Michelangelo's assignment might have been easier had Pope Julius II been a more understanding man. But he was not. He was headstrong and impatient and constantly badgered Michelangelo to hurry the project. He wanted the paintings completed during his lifetime. Even though he was an old man, the pope often climbed a ladder to the top of the scaffold and berated his frustrated artist. Once, having grown tired of Michelangelo answering his question "How much longer?" with his usual "As soon as I can," Julius gave him a smart whack with his staff. He even threatened to have Michelangelo thrown off the scaffold if he didn't hurry!

In spite of the pope's prodding, it took Michelangelo more than four years to complete the chapel ceiling. He often worked around the clock, skipping meals and napping in his clothes. The scenes he painted were frescoes, which are paintings done on wet plaster. Paint constantly dripped in his face, and his eyesight suffered from the strain of focusing on his work. Even his ability to freely move his neck was affected. After four years of lying on his back, he could only read a letter by holding the page above his head and looking upward.

Michelangelo finished the Sistine ceiling amidst great fanfare in 1512. Twenty-two years later, he began the *Last Judgment* on the end wall of the chapel. It was a project that took him eight years to complete. Although not part of the original ceiling paintings, many critics consider *Last Judgment* Michelangelo's greatest work of art. Michelangelo also designed the great dome of the Church of St. Peter's in Rome. He was active until the time of his death in 1564.

Michelangelo, like Leonardo da Vinci, was so obsessed with portraying the human form accurately that he too dissected and studied countless bodies to make his paintings and sculptures as realistic as possible. His quest for perfection was characteristic of the artists of the Renaissance.

The Last Judgment, one of nine scenes from the biblical book of Genesis painted by Michelangelo on the ceiling of the Sistine Chapel in Rome.

Name _____ Date _____

Solve Some Sistine Chapel Math

Below are three word problems dealing with the Sistine Chapel in Rome. Work each in the space provided and write its answer on the given line. Use the equivalency data below in solving the problems.

10.76 square feet = 1 square meter

1. a. The Sistine Chapel measures 132 feet by 45 feet. Therefore, the chapel contains _____ square feet.

   b. Convert the number of square feet above into square meters. In doing so, you will find that the chapel contains _____ square meters. (Round your answer.)

2. The ceiling of the Sistine Chapel painted by Michelangelo covers about 3,000 square feet. How many square meters does the ceiling cover? _____ square meters. (Round your answer.)

3. Michelangelo's *Last Judgment* is a fresco that covers about 200 square feet on the end wall of the Sistine Chapel. How many square meters does the painting cover? _____ square meters

From *Everyday Life: The Renaissance* © 2005 Good Year Books.

Name _____ Date _____

Use Context Clues to Complete Sentences

Fill in the blanks in the sentences using the words from the word box.

accomplished
agree
attest
construction
contributions
drew
excelled
greater
models
modern
primarily
produced
second
statues
study
unsurpassed

The Renaissance _____ many great artists, but none were _____ than Leonardo da Vinci and Michelangelo Buonarroti. Both were multi-talented individuals who _____ in a number of areas. Although Leonardo was _____ a painter and Michelangelo considered himself above all a sculptor, each made _____ in other fields as well.

Leonardo da Vinci is mostly remembered for two paintings. They are the *Last Supper* and the *Mona Lisa.* But he also was an _____ sculptor and engineer. He _____ designs for bridges and highways, as well as for a diving bell and tank. _____ engineers have used drawings from his notebooks and made working _____ of machines he proposed centuries ago. Not the least of his achievements was the knowledge of anatomy he acquired from his _____ of the human body.

Some people think Michelangelo was even more gifted than Leonardo. His _____ of David and Moses and his *Pietá* are _____ in detail and beauty. As a painter, the scenes he painted on the ceiling of the Sistine Chapel in Rome _____ to his talent with the brush. And as an architect, his skills were _____ to none. In his later years, he designed plans for the _____ of St. Peter's Church in Rome.

Don't you _____ that Leonardo da Vinci and Michelangelo Buonarotti were two very talented individuals?

Name _____ Date _____

Write a Lead Paragraph for *The Rome Review*

Suppose that newspapers existed in 1512 and you are a reporter for *The Rome Review*. Your assignment is to write a story covering Michelangelo's completion of the paintings on the ceiling of the Sistine Chapel in Rome.

On the lines provided, write the lead paragraph to that story that would go along with the headline given. Be sure to included answers to the five "W" questions (Who? What? When? Where? Why?) that are characteristic of a good lead paragraph.

The Rome Review

✶ ✶ ✶ ✶ ✶ November 1, 1512 ✶ ✶ ✶ ✶ ✶

Michelangelo Completes Paintings at Sistine Chapel

Four Years of Hard Work Over

_____
_____
_____
_____
_____
_____
_____
_____
_____
_____
_____
_____
_____
_____
_____
_____
_____
_____

From *Everyday Life: The Renaissance* © 2005 Good Year Books.

Name _____ Date _____

Make a Sketch

In the space provided, make a sketch of a drawing from Leonardo da Vinci's notebooks. You can find samples by looking in any encyclopedia or biography of Leonardo.

On the lines at the bottom of the page, tell about the drawing you have chosen to copy.

_____

_____

_____

_____

_____

_____

CHAPTER 4

Marriage and Home Life

The Renaissance caused Europeans to think differently about life and the world around them. First in Italy and then elsewhere, people began to focus on happiness in this life instead of dwelling on death and the hereafter. It would seem natural, then, that their ideas about other things—such as the position of women in society—would change too. But that was not the case. In the Renaissance, women for the most part were still considered inferior to men. Their place was at home taking care of children and household duties. It is true that some educated women and those from the leading noble families rose to prominence. Such women moved in all circles of society and influenced many fields of Renaissance life. Some ruled states and nations and succeeded as well as any of their male counterparts. A few even wore armor and accompanied their husbands onto the battlefield. A woman of education or of the upper classes found many doors open to her during the Renaissance.

The life of Catherine Sforza tells us a great deal about how upper-class and noble women lived during the Renaissance. Catherine was the countess of Forli and Imola, two cities in northern Italy. Her husband was Girolamo Riario, the despot (absolute ruler) of Forli. Girolamo was so cruel that his subjects rebelled in 1487 and assassinated him. Catherine, who was nine months pregnant, set out with a group of loyal troops and captured the rebel leader. The next day, she gave birth to a child. How's that for one brave and determined woman?

Renaissance Europe, however, had few Catherine Sforzas. Most women were housewives and mothers first and foremost. For them life was different. If they excelled at book learning, they were expected to keep quiet and not flaunt it. Their husbands were advised to keep them quiet and obedient.

Catherine Sforza, a unique woman of the Renaissance.

From *Everyday Life: The Renaissance* © 2005 Good Year Books.

For both the rich and the poor, marriage during the Renaissance had very little to do with love. Marriage centered around property and the bride's dowry, a gift of money or property she brought to her husband at marriage. Families arranged all betrothals (engagements), and most young people accepted the mates chosen for them. The best they could hope for was that love might come later. Often it did, as couples drew closer together through the trials and tribulations of marriage and parenthood.

Girls were often betrothed as young as 3, though marriage did not come until the age of 12. Any girl not married by the time she was 15 was a disgrace to her family. Still, many girls never wed because their families could not afford a dowry. A few determined ones in places such as Florence could, if they had the means, buy state dowry insurance. That way, by paying yearly premiums, they could in time build up a dowry to offer a prospective husband.

Men put off marriage as long as possible. This was because society permitted them more freedom in their relations with women. In the minds of many, marriage for men was unnecessary. During the Renaissance, there was no stigma

Renaissance newlyweds. A candle burning in a daylit room was part of the traditional ceremony.

attached to an unmarried man as there was to an unmarried woman. Some of the most famous men of the day never had wives. Neither Raphael, Michelangelo, nor Leonardo da Vinci ever married. Bachelors delayed marriage to the point that, in an effort to get more bachelors to marry, some cities passed laws forbidding men between the ages of 20 and 50 from holding public office unless they were married.

Even though men put off getting married during the Renaissance, a wife and children were looked upon by society as the true source of happiness in

life. A happy home was considered more important than fame and fortune. Renaissance people believed that a man, however, should marry a woman much younger than he so he could mold and train her as he saw fit. The age difference would also give the husband plenty of time to teach his wife how to properly manage a household.

When a man of the upper class did marry, an enormous sum was usually spent on the wedding. It was not unusual for a noble or upper-class family to spend half a million dollars at the event. No expense or effort was spared in making weddings social extravaganzas. One Italian nobleman entertained 30,000 guests during his wedding celebration. Another brought his lovely bride home to Florence and was greeted by the upper-class women and children of the city, who sang a cantata especially written for the occasion.

Despite the fact that Renaissance women were still lowly members of society and that men delayed marriage as long as possible, the Renaissance family was a close-knit and loving group. Parents and children cared for one another in both upper-class and lower-class settings. Servants and apprentices lived with their masters and were treated as family members.

As a rule, Renaissance families were large. Women had many children, but many babies died in childbirth or early infancy. Widowers might remarry a number of times, bringing their children from previous marriages into the extended family. Leonardo da Vinci, for example, had several stepmothers and 16 half-brothers and half-sisters. Children born to their fathers out of wedlock were also accepted into the family. No one thought to treat them any differently than the other children.

During the Renaissance, the father of the family was supreme. He did not hold the power of life and death over his family as in some ancient societies, but what he said was taken as law. Still, it was the mother who ruled the household whether at a villa (country estate), town house, or on a peasant farm. The mother supervised the daily activities of the home. She saw to the milling of flour and to the baking of bread. She made certain that the vineyards—so important for making wine—were taken care of properly. She checked to be sure that all meat had been salted for preservation. If she belonged to the nobility or the upper class, in the absence of her husband she might also supervise the affairs of state until his return.

What kind of homes did Renaissance wives help supervise? For one thing, they were usually sparsely furnished. This was true for both the upper class and the common people. Chairs, tables, benches, and chests were the main

From *Everyday Life: The Renaissance* © 2005 Good Year Books.

furnishings. Chairs were hard and uncomfortable, and some time would pass before they were padded with cushions.

There were exceptions, of course. Some of the palaces and villas of nobles and wealthy businessmen in Italy were luxurious. Floors might be of marble or tile and rooms decorated with ornate columns and pilasters. (A pilaster is a decorative column built into a wall.) Expensive carpets and beautiful drapes might adorn every room, along with comfortable beds and perfumed linen. Huge fireplaces with sculptured mantels warmed every room in the house.

Until the 1200s, fireplaces were located in the center of a room. Smoke filled the entire living space and made it very uncomfortable for those within. At the beginning of the Renaissance, architects designed houses in which the fireplaces were moved to the walls and were connected to chimneys that directed the smoke out of the house.

The location of the fireplace along a wall also made cooking easier. Large pots could be suspended from chains and raised or lowered to adjust the cooking temperature. Frying pans with long handles made it possible to cook other meals over the hottest part of the fire. Cooking over a fireplace was the rule everywhere until the middle of the 1600s, when the first stoves came into use.

The foods Renaissance families cooked over their fireplaces are discussed in chapter 5, "Fashion and Food."

A typical hard chair of Renaissance times. Padded chairs did not come into use until the seventeenth century.

Name _____ Date _____

Use Your Critical-Thinking Skills

Think about the four questions below and write your best answers on the lines provided.

1. What impact did education have on a Renaissance woman's life?

   _____
   _____
   _____

2. In your opinion, what percent of men today still think a woman's place is "in the home"? What are your personal feelings?

   _____
   _____
   _____

3. For what reasons were young girls betrothed at such tender ages during the Renaissance?

   _____
   _____
   _____

4. Think for a moment about a 12-year-old Renaissance girl who is about to be married. What thoughts might be racing through her head as she prepares for the wedding? Do you think she is happy? Sad? Has she accepted her fate as beyond her control?

   _____
   _____
   _____
   _____
   _____
   _____

Name _____ Date _____

Fill in a Venn Diagram

Fill in the Venn diagram to compare marriage during the Renaissance period with marriage today. Write facts about each in the appropriate place. List features common to both where the circles overlap.

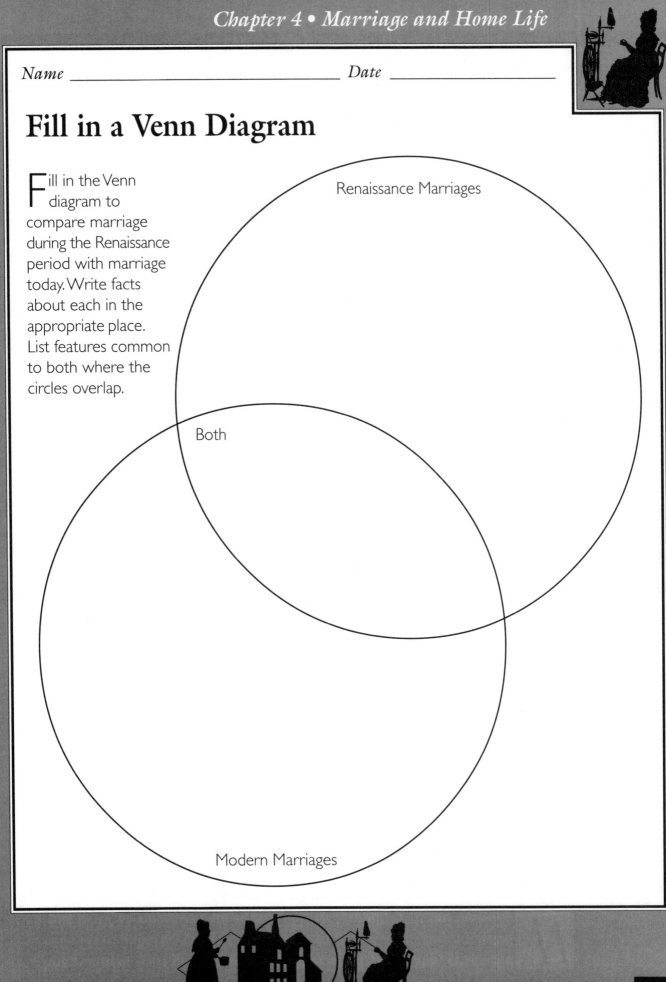

Renaissance Marriages

Both

Modern Marriages

Name _____ Date _____

Solve Wedding-Related Math

The Duke of Anjou is getting married. In addition to the local nobility from Nantes who will attend the wedding, guests throughout France have been invited. The number of out-of-town guests who are expected to attend are listed here beside their respective provinces.

Review mean, median, mode, and range in your math book and answer these questions. Space is provided for you to work each one.

Province	Number of Guests
Brittany	200
Champagne	165
Gascony	182
Lorraine	210
Nice	165
Normandy	413
Burgundy	86

1. How many out-of-town guests are expected to attend the duke's wedding? _____

2. What is the mean number of those who will attend? _____

3. What number represents the median? _____

4. What is the range? _____

5. Is a mode represented in the numbers above? If so, what is it? _____

From Everyday Life: The Renaissance © 2005 Good Year Books.

Name _____ Date _____

Complete a Word Search

In the word box are 20 words taken from chapter 4. Find and circle each in the word search. They run horizontally, vertically, and diagonally. None are inverted or backward.

```
E X Z E R V K L P M C V W S O
X Y W E D D I N G B A K L O T
T M C R O Y A L C D N N F C T
R G O H W C A T L Q T R T I U
A E U G R S T U V A A B B E H
V I N E Y A R D K P T L L L L
A B T A C D H P S P A U U Y V
G E E F I J O E K R L L M B G
A B S C D S U A F E F H A A Z
N O S M N T S S T N V V R C D
C H A I R I E A Z T K Z R H E
E T R A L G H N N I K K I E C
S T O R M M O T T C K G A L Z
S U E I T A L Y B E E T G O T
D A D D Y Z D W I D O W E R K
```

APPRENTICE
BACHELOR
CANTATA
COUNTESS
DOWRY
EXTRAVAGANCE
HOUSEHOLD
ITALY
MANTEL
MARRIAGE
PALACE
PEASANT
RENAISSANCE
ROYAL
SOCIETY
STIGMA
VILLA
VINEYARD
WEDDING
WIDOWER

CHAPTER 5

Fashion and Food

Imagine a group of people from Renaissance Europe standing on a street corner in Anywhere, U.S.A., today. As they watch the people walk by, they point and giggle. Pierced ears? Pierced lips, noses, and tongues? And what about all those tattooes gracing arms and other body parts? These people are really weird, they would probably think!

But hold on a minute. If a group of modern people traveled back in time to Renaissance Europe, they would have the same reaction. Curls and braids glued to various parts of the head? Hair arranged in the form of figure eights? And what about the men walking around in tight, colored hose? Talk about weird, our group of moderns might think!

Every period of history is famous for fashions and fads unique to it alone. Sometimes fashions and fads carry over to the succeeding century; sometimes they swing back and forth. Such is the case, for example, with men's hairstyles. In the 1300s, men of all classes wore their hair long and turned up in a roll at the ears, with bangs hanging down their foreheads. As the Renaissance period progressed, however, long hair went out of style in favor of the shorter variety. The same was true of facial hair. At times beards were in; at other times all men were clean shaven. Other aspects of fashion have passed through similar changes.

In discussing Renaissance fashion, where better to begin than with women's hairstyles? Renaissance women, especially those of the upper classes, devoted a good deal of time to arranging, decorating, and coloring their hair. The methods they used are interesting.

One type of hairstyle favored by noble women of the Renaissance.

Renaissance women preferred blonde hair color. Those not so lucky as to have been born that way went to great lengths to achieve the same result. Some simply dyed their hair. Others spent whole days in the sun hoping to bleach their tresses. Still others used gold lacquer to create a hair color referred to as "Venus's hair." (Venus was the Roman goddess of love and beauty.)

From Everyday Life: The Renaissance © 2005 Good Year Books.

The desire of upper-class women to change their hair color proved a windfall for their peasant counterparts. Many peasant women would cut their long, blonde hair and sell it to ladies of the noble and wealthy classes. These ladies then glued the hairpieces onto their heads with a substance called *gum arabic*. Some wealthy women even had entire wigs made of white or yellow silk, although such false hair was forbidden by law in some places.

Women wore various headdresses during the 300-year Renaissance period. These ranged from simple caps like those worn by boys to elaborate tiaras and turbans. They also wore pillbox-type hats and the "steeple" hats associated with the Middle Ages. High, square headdresses became fashionable in England, as did "butterfly" headdresses supported by wires. Because hats varied from country to country and changed with each century, no one headdress can be identified as purely Renaissance.

Once the Renaissance lady was satisfied with her hair and head covering, she might put on a dress of heavy velvet that reached to the floor and was bound at the waist by a girdle or sash. The sleeves of her dress were often decorated with gold and silver embroidery, and her petticoat was trimmed with lace and embroidered with silk. Because streets were filthy and often muddy, women of the Renaissance wore shoes with high heels and high soles.

Although the Renaissance lady looked like she stepped out of a picture book, her clothing must have been uncomfortable. Her dress often included a ruff, a stiff white collar that reached to the neck and sometimes over the head. To attain an "hourglass" figure, she wore a corset that could be tightened by pulling on laces. In the late 1500s women began to wear farthingales. These were heavy metal frames that made skirts stand out and gave a woman the appearance of walking in a box. Special chairs with no arms were needed for a woman in a farthingale to sit down.

Jewelry of every type was popular with Renaissance upper classes. Women and men wore rings, bracelets, necklaces, and earrings studded with diamonds, pearls, rubies, sapphires, and other precious gems. It was the same with perfumes. Hair, shirts, hats, stockings, gloves, and shoes were doused in perfume. Rouge was also popular, being applied liberally to the face, neck, chest, and other parts of the body.

Renaissance men were equally fastidious in dress. They wore long, colored stockings and short padded tunics. Beneath a doublet, or jacket, they wore shirts of linen or silk decorated with lace and wide ruffled sleeves. Gloves and shoes were ornate too. Depending on location, men's hats were broad-rimmed

and decorated with jewels and ostrich feathers. And, yes, men also used perfumes. One Italian gentleman wrote to another thanking him because the money he received in payment for a debt had been scented with perfume.

Peasants, of course, did not wear fancy clothes or jewelry and they certainly did not douse themselves in perfume. In most places, laws forbid them to do so. Instead, peasant dress was simple. Women wore a loose garment of wool with a hood that completely covered the head. Usually their clothing was dyed a dull green or brown, as bright colors were reserved for people of rank. Peasant men usually wore a one-piece garment tucked up into their belt. In place of shoes, they wore stockings made of soft cloth and had stiff soles. Men and women wore wooden shoes or clogs when working in the fields. The poorest people went barefoot.

A man sports a doublet, a close-fitting jacket that was part of a Renaissance gentleman's costume.

Fashions and styles popular at the end of the Renaissance were the same as those of colonial America. What the Spanish, French, English, Dutch, and others wore in Europe, they wore in their colonies. Children's dress followed adult styles. Because children were viewed as small adults, their clothing was similar to that of their parents. Boys and girls wore dresses until about the age of seven or eight. Then, boys took to wearing a version of men's clothing. Young girls wore the same uncomfortable dresses as their mothers, complete with a stiff ruff at the neck. Clothing for children remained impractical until well into the 1900s.

Foods consumed during the Renaissance period varied from place to place. Wheat, wine, olives, and olive oil were the basic foods in Italy, Spain, and southern France. The English enjoyed pies, tarts, puddings, and such meats as venison, pork, beef, mutton, and chicken. The French, the Spanish, and others had their own special dishes. All nationalities, regardless of what was set on the table before them, shunned water, which was usually unfit to drink. The French drank wine, the English ale, and the Germans beer.

What Europeans ate changed considerably during the Age of Exploration and Discovery, which began in the 1400s. New foods were introduced that people never knew existed. Chief among these were corn, sweet and white potatoes, squash, and tomatoes. Turkeys were brought to Europe from the

From *Everyday Life: The Renaissance* © 2005 Good Year Books.

West Indies. These large fowl were so-called because Columbus and others had mistakenly taken the New World for Asia, of which Turkey was considered a part.

Just because a new food was brought to Europe did not mean Europeans took to it immediately. The potato, which was brought to Spain from South America about 1570, was not widely grown in Europe until the 1700s. The same was true of the tomato. Europeans rejected this strange, red vegetable because they thought it was poisonous. The Italians finally began to eat tomatoes near the end of the Renaissance, but it was much later before other Europeans followed suit. (The tomato was not eaten in America until the 1800s, when a man in New Jersey ate one before a horrified crowd. When he did not drop dead because of his "foolishness," the tomato slowly caught on.)

One other change in the dining habits of Europeans is worthy of mention. That was the introduction of the fork in Italy in the 1400s. As you already know, people ate with their fingers. They wiped their hands on a napkin or tablecloth and sometimes even on their clothes. The advent of the fork caused people to improve their table manners. It also meant fewer greasy clothes in the family laundry basket.

Who could have imagined that the simple fork would have such a profound effect on European society?

Several kinds of foods that appeared in Europe for the first time during the Renaissance.

Name _____ Date _____

Sketch a Costume

You have learned that dress during the Renaissance varied from country to country and from century to century.

In the space provided, draw a picture illustrating either a man's or a woman's attire at some point in the Renaissance. You can find examples by looking through a book dealing with the period or by looking under "Clothing" in an encyclopedia. Color your illustration to make it more authentic and indicate beneath it the century and the country (if applicable) it represents.

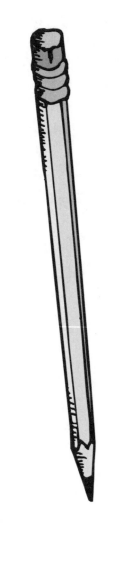

From Everyday Life: The Renaissance © 2005 Good Year Books.

Name _____ Date _____

Match Foods and Countries

Many foods eaten by people during the Renaissance found their way to America in the 1600s. Others were introduced later by immigrants from many different lands.

In the column to the left are 20 foods that have become American favorites. Match each correctly with the country with which it is associated. Some countries are used more than once.

_____ 1. crêpes suzette

_____ 2. chow mein

_____ 3. escargots

_____ 4. fish and chips

_____ 5. frankfurter

_____ 6. goulash

_____ 7. hamburger

_____ 8. meat pies

_____ 9. moo goo gai pan

_____ 10. moussaka

_____ 11. pizza

_____ 12. ravioli

_____ 13. sauerkraut

_____ 14. shish kebab

_____ 15. spaghetti

_____ 16. strudel

_____ 17. sukiyaki

_____ 18. sushi

_____ 19. taco

_____ 20. tortilla

A. China

B. England

C. France

D. Germany

E. Greece

F. Hungary

G. Italy

H. Japan

I. Mexico

J. Turkey

Name _____ Date _____

Write a Blurb for a Book on Clothing

Are you familiar with the word *blurb*? A blurb is a complimentary advertisement or announcement, such as appears on the jacket of a book. Its purpose is to praise the book and influence people to buy it.

Imagine you have just read a book on Renaissance clothing. On the lines provided, write a blurb summarizing its contents.

From *Everyday Life: The Renaissance* © 2005 Good Year Books.

Name _____ Date _____

Solve a Fashion and Food Puzzle

ACROSS

1 Gave women an hourglass figure

5 Man's jacket

9 Metal frame worn beneath skirts

12 Beverage drunk by Germans

13 Eating implement

14 Fabric worn by peasant women

15 Roman goddess of love and beauty

DOWN

2 Vegetable thought to be poisonous

3 Stiff white collar

4 Preferred hair color of the Renaissance

6 Headdress supported by wires

7 What Europeans seldom drank

8 French mealtime beverage

10 Gum _____

11 Large fowl imported into Europe from the West Indies

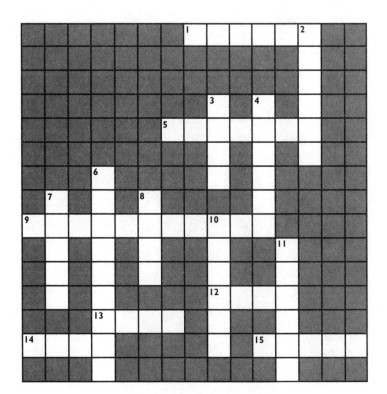

Fun and Amusements

For the most part, Renaissance people were fun-loving. You have already learned how Leonardo da Vinci once livened up a party by fashioning balloons from the entrails of a ram. While most Renaissance people were not as creative as Leonardo, they nevertheless saw any occasion as cause to fill the streets with singing and merrymaking.

Some forms of Renaissance entertainment were carryovers from the Middle Ages. People still played chess and, in some places, continued to cheer on knights jousting at tournaments. Although feudalism had all but ended, there were still enough knights around to provide a lively bout for thrill-seekers. Sometimes streets of towns were roped off and the rambunctious participants had a go at it. Such jousts were usually staged beneath balconies and open windows to allow the ladies of the town an opportunity to cheer for their favorite contestants.

When jousts failed to satisfy some of the more bloodthirsty observers, new amusements were introduced. In 1332, a group of young daredevils introduced bullfighting in the old Roman Colosseum. The result of this event was catastrophic.

Young men of Florence engage in a type of boxing called *civettino.* Civettino differed from traditional boxing in that a boxer could pin down his opponent by standing on his feet.

Since the "matadors" were men on foot armed only with spears, the bulls easily came out on top. Had there been a scoreboard at each end of the Colosseum that day, it might have read something like: "Bulls 18, Knights 11." In time, the Spanish adopted bullfighting as their national pastime.

Although bullfighting never caught on in Italy, other sports did. One was a crude kind of football that, like chess and jousting, carried over from the Middle Ages. Sometimes each team consisted of up to 27 players. With so many rough young men chasing after the same ball, it is easy to imagine the number of black eyes and broken bones that occurred.

In addition to football, competitive sports included boxing and tennis. Boxing as performed in Renaissance Italy is especially interesting. It was called *civettino* and differed considerably from traditional boxing. In civettino, a boxer tried to pin down his opponent by standing on one of his feet. He then flailed away with punches and jabs until his adversary cried for quarter.

From *Everyday Life: The Renaissance* © 2005 Good Year Books.

A favorite pastime of all Europeans was watching and participating in festivals and carnivals. As mentioned earlier, almost any important occasion was considered worthy of celebration. The occasion might be the anniversary of some important event, such as a great victory on the battlefield or the signing of a welcomed peace. It might be the crowning of a new ruler or the visit of a foreign dignitary. Usually, however, it was one of many religious and state holidays that gave people a break from their daily routines and concerns.

City processions were popular. In these early parades, thousands dressed in their best finery and marched to the beat of lively music. Nobles, clergymen, and leading citizens might lead the way, followed by the likes of musicians, acrobats, and jesters. There were also horse-drawn floats built in the forms of various animals and decorated in brilliant colors. And, like present-day parades that feature majorettes and flag twirlers, these processions included pretty girls who sang and danced along the way. The evening's festivities often ended with a brilliant fireworks display.

Peasants in the German city of Nuremberg dance in the market square during a festival.

Carnivals were even higher on the Renaissance person's entertainment list. A carnival was a celebration usually held just before the beginning of Lent, a period of some 40 days before Easter. Lent was a time dedicated to fasting and penitence, and a carnival afforded people a chance to celebrate and "blow off steam" before it began. On carnival nights, everybody donned masks and played pranks. People of all ranks and classes joined in the fun.

One of the best-known carnivals was Mardi Gras. Mardi Gras is a French term meaning "Fat Tuesday." The term is derived from the custom of revelers parading a fat pig through the streets on Shrove Tuesday, the day before Lent begins. Mardi Gras is still celebrated today in a cities throughout the world. Chief among these in the United States are New Orleans, Louisiana; Mobile, Alabama; and Biloxi, Mississippi.

From *Everyday Life: The Renaissance* © 2005 Good Year Books.

Mardi Gras-type carnivals were also held elsewhere during the Renaissance. In Germany, the event was called Fasnacht, and in England, Pancake Tuesday. Pancake Tuesday must have been an interesting event. On that day, housewives made pancakes and met in the village square. At a given signal, they raced toward the village church, each being required to flip a hot pancake on the griddle three times before reaching the church door. The winner received a special blessing from the parish caretaker. Pancake Tuesday is still a tradition in some English villages today.

Members of the nobility participating in one of their favorite pastimes: hunting. Bringing along sizable amounts of wine and food, they turned the hunt into a major outing.

When there were no festivals or carnivals on the calendar, Renaissance people occupied themselves with other amusements. Races of all types drew large crowds. There were foot races, boat regattas, and horse races. The latter often took place in city streets and sent passersby scurrying for cover. Spectators were sometimes injured and riders thrown and trampled in these wild contests.

Card playing and gambling with dice were other entertainment passions. Men of rank gambled and lost huge fortunes at the card and dice tables. The situation was so severe in some places that legislation was passed forbidding the sale of cards and dice altogether. Servants were even encouraged to report masters who played and gambled on the sly. Chronic gamblers who sought loans might be turned down unless they signed a pledge promising not to gamble until the loan was repaid.

Hunting was another pastime that occupied people, especially the upper classes. Hunts were colossal affairs that often lasted for weeks. They were organized by official huntsmen, who saw that no detail was overlooked. Sometimes entire courts took part and huge amounts of food and wine were brought along to cater to their needs. The usual prey in these hunts were deer or boar, although birds and small animals were still hunted with falcons as in the Middle Ages.

Hunting was a fast-paced endeavor. The huntsmen led the participants, blowing on a horn when game was spotted. At the sound of his blast, the avid participants charged forward at full speed. Henry VIII, who ruled England from 1509 to 1547, was said to have worn out eight horses in a single day's hunting. Usually men engaged in royal and noble hunts, but some women found them exciting as well. Elizabeth I of England, who ruled from 1558–1603, was known to have been an avid fan of the hunt.

From *Everyday Life: The Renaissance* © 2005 Good Year Books.

Even popes found time to amuse themselves. Leo X, who headed the Roman Catholic Church from 1513 to 1522, was a happy-go-lucky leader who relished life and entertainment. He enjoyed hunting and had a large number of horses and about 100 grooms to care for them. In addition to hunting, Leo often played cards with high church officials before large crowds of spectators. He also kept jesters and buffoons (clowns) at the Vatican for his amusement. Some sources maintain that Leo enjoyed nothing more than seeing one of his buffoons swallow 40 eggs in succession!

Finally, there were lavish parties where privileged men and women dressed in fancy clothes and were entertained by musicians in masks and elaborate costumes. Often the highlight of such gatherings was a play put on by a troupe of actors. The play itself or the talent of the actors was sometimes less important than the scenery and the between-the-act shenanigans. Fireworks might be set off during breaks in the play, or several cooks who had had a little too much to drink might dance about the stage beating on pots. And sometimes, to the delight of all those in attendance, the actors would set fire to the scenery!

Name _____ Date _____

Interpret a Pie Graph

Lavish parties were a favorite pastime of the upper classes of Renaissance Europe. At such parties guests were entertained by musicians, actors, wrestlers, acrobats, and jesters.

Suppose that one such party was attended by 120 people. After the party, each person was asked to name his or her favorite group of performers. Some would say they liked the musicians best, while others would vote in favor of the actors or one of the other groups.

The graph below is a sampling showing the percentage of guests that favored each group. Use the figures from the graph to answer the question at the bottom of the page.

Party Guests' Preferences

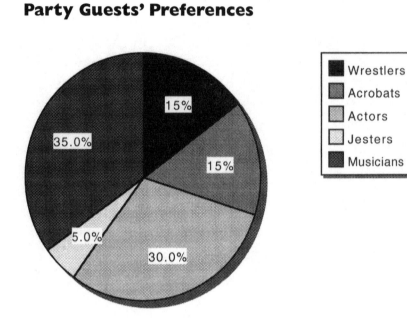

Legend:
- Wrestlers
- Acrobats
- Actors
- Jesters
- Musicians

15%
35.0%
15%
5.0%
30.0%

Determine the number of partygoers that favored each of the following:

1. Jesters _____

2. Musicians _____

3. Wrestlers _____

4. Actors _____

5. Acrobats _____

Name _____ Date _____

Conduct a Survey

Conduct a survey of at least 20 people as to their three favorite kinds of recreation and/or entertainment. You may include fellow students, family members, and neighborhood friends.

When you have completed your survey, make a chart on the lines below to show your findings

_____

_____

_____

_____

_____

_____

_____

_____

_____

_____

_____

_____

_____

_____

_____

_____

Name _____ Date _____

Indicate Which Word Does Not Belong

To the right are groups of words associated in some way with recreation and entertainment. All but a few were mentioned in chapter 6.

Underline the one word in each group that does not belong. Then, on the line below, explain why it is out of place.

1. hounds   helmets   horns   hunters

   _____

2. rook   pawn   serf   knight

   _____

3. lance   armor   horse   lute

   _____

4. ball   matador   bull   stadium

   _____

5. cards   dice   roulette   dominoes

   _____

6. bands   floats   fireworks   majorettes

   _____

7. advisor   singer   acrobat   jester

   _____

8. Mardi Gras   All Saints Day   Pancake Tuesday   Fasnacht

   _____

9. football   basketball   soccer   tennis

   _____

10. New Orleans   Florida   Biloxi   Mobile

   _____

From Everyday Life: The Renaissance © 2005 GoodYear Books.

Name _____   Date _____

Make a Shoe-Box Diorama

Make a shoe-box diorama depicting a form of recreation or entertainment popular in Renaissance times. You might want to create one of the following scenes:

1. a procession or parade commemorating some holiday or event

2. a party hosted by a member of the upper class

3. a royal hunt

4. a kind of Renaissance boxing

5. a horse race

6. a street scene from a carnival such as Mardi Gras

7. a joust between two knights on horseback

Or, you may want to think of a scene of your own to create.

Some of the materials you will need are:

1. A large shoe box

2. Construction paper

3. Cardboard

4. Markers or watercolors and paintbrush

5. Glue or paste

6. Modeling clay or small figurines of people and animals

7. Scissors

Manners and Behavior

It was the best of times, it was the worst of times, it was the age of wisdom, it was the age of foolishness . . .

Y ou are probably not familiar with the above statement, but your teacher may recognize it as the beginning of Charles Dickens's *A Tale of Two Cities*. Dickens wrote this famous novel of the French Revolution published in 1859, and it has remained a classic ever since.

The words with which Dickens began *A Tale of Two Cities* could be used to describe a number of periods in history. Even the history of the United States contains a time of such extremes. For example, we refer to the years between the Reconstruction Era and the turn of the twentieth century by many names: the Golden Nineties, the Gilded Age, and the Age of Steel and Steam. Above all, it might best be called the Age of Extremes. It was an age of great wealth and great poverty in the United States. This was a time when America advertised for immigrants and then discriminated against them once they arrived. It was an age of booming cities and ugly slums. Progress in one area was balanced by neglect in another.

The beginning of *A Tale of Two Cities* could just as easily describe the Renaissance period. You have learned that it was an age of great achievement in art and other fields; a time when people focused more on this life than on the next. On the surface, it was a happy era when Europeans broke out of the doldrums of the Middle Ages. It was also a time of petty quarrels and much violence. Family feuds and conflicts between city-states and between rulers of nations began over the slightest insult and went on for generations. And, in spite of the decline of feudalism, travel in some places remained extremely hazardous.

While Renaissance people might be petty and sometimes violent, they could also be splendid in their dress and impeccable in their personal hygiene, conversation, and table manners. The Italian states ranked first in the fine art of social behavior, with Florence leading the way. The Italians, in fact, considered other Europeans to be coarse and unrefined. They bathed frequently (a rarity at the time) and ate with forks, as you have already seen. And you probably remember from chapter 5 how particular they were about their dress.

How did Italians know what was proper and what was frowned on when it came to manners and etiquette? First, they could rush to their local bookseller

and purchase the latest book on behavior from a bookseller. Behavior books were popular during the Renaissance and were designed to teach people how to act in every social situation. Separate books were written for the upper and middle classes. The lower classes seemed to have set their own standards of behavior without the aid of any book.

The most influential of the behavior books was *The Courtier,* or *Il Cortegiano,* written by Baldassare Castiglione for the Italian upper classes. It was also widely read in other parts of Europe. In *The Courtier,* Castiglione counsels "gentlemen" as to their proper relationship with inferiors. In short, he warns them to associate with people of lesser birth as little as possible. When they have to on occasion, they must always remain aloof and maintain their position of dignity. Perhaps with tongue in cheek, he states that a gentleman should not wrestle with a peasant unless he is sure of winning. Nothing would be more humiliating than a gentleman of rank being body-slammed to the ground by a lowly farm boy!

Many Renaissance behavior books dealt with the family and education. The aim of education was to develop character and prepare children (mostly boys) for the outside world of business and politics. Not only was a young man taught to succeed in a chosen profession, he was instructed in the fine art of conversation. Renaissance nobility considered good conversational skills crucial, and no one was looked down on more than a boring talker. Above all, the good conversationalist was expected to focus on matters of interest to his associates and refrain from talking too much about his wife and children.

Giovanni della Casa, another Italian writer, published a book on manners. Della Casa admonished readers not to grind or suck their teeth because such noises "grate upon the ear." And even though the book was written near the end of the Renaissance, he cautioned the gentleman at the table not to wipe his fingers on his bread or even to get his napkin too dirty. Such behavior, he pointed out, might have an adverse affect on the appetites of his fellow diners.

Federigo da Montefeltro, the Duke of Urbino, was typical of Baldassare Castiglione's "gentleman," which he described in his book of behavior, *The Courtier.*

From Everyday Life: The Renaissance © 2005 GoodYear Books.

Della Casa went further in his drive to eliminate crudeness at the table. He stated that it was unmannerly for a gentleman to sniff the contents of another's cup or smell the meat he was about to eat for fear that "some drop from his nose" might fall onto either. On a less gross note, he counseled that it was just as unrefined to sip wine from a friend's glass or offer him a piece of fruit from which a bite or two had already been taken.

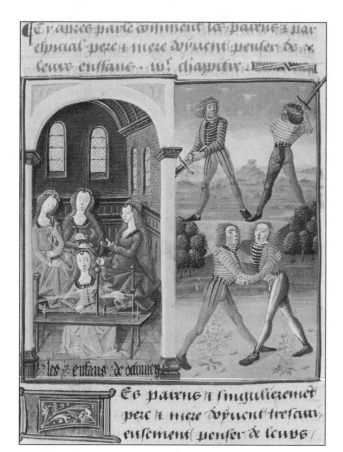

A partial list of rules from *The Book of Manners,* written in the sixteenth century by Giovanni della Casa.

Della Casa, like Castiglione, also offered advice about conversation. He stated that a man should neither talk too slowly nor too fast, either of which could be viewed with distaste by his listener. He also added that no man, while talking, should come so close to another's face that his breath might prove offensive. In an age when no one understood tooth decay and most people had lost all their teeth by the age of 30, the latter was no doubt wise counsel.

The many conduct books that circulated throughout Europe prove just how contradictory Renaissance behavior was. People could be tender and caring while at the same time cruel and violent. As mentioned at the beginning of the chapter, feuds flourished and duels were the accepted way to settle disputes. Anyone who did not have the stomach for dueling could always enlist the help of an assassin or a maker of poisons. Differences were often settled with knives. It was an age when people seldom sat down to try to resolve conflicts in a peaceful manner.

There were also books that dealt with safety in such a time of lawlessness. People were warned to stay indoors after dark. If for some reason they had to venture out at night, they were advised to carry a good light and to go in the company of a friend. Never, they were further cautioned, should they let their destination be known to others outside their family and close acquaintances. If they were going in one direction, they should spread a rumor that they were really going in the opposite.

From *Everyday Life: The Renaissance* © 2005 Good Year Books.

Travel was as unsafe in the country as in the city. Everyone ran the risk of being attacked by robbers and mercenaries. Mercenary soldiers abounded in Italy, where the various city-states hired outsiders to fight their wars for them. When there were no wars to fight, mercenaries sometimes obtained their "pay" by attacking helpless travelers on desolate roads. Such blood-thirsty bandits easily overwhelmed any armed escort hired by the travelers. Usually they killed their victims and stole their possessions, although sometimes they held them for ransom.

A painting by Italian artist Giovanni Bellini, *The Murder of St. Peter the Martyr,* goes far to illustrate the violence of the times. It also shows how accustomed onlookers were to attacks on hapless people. In the painting, two travelers are being set upon by two mercenaries with knives. In the woods in the immediate background, five woodcutters go about their work, obviously caring little for the plight of the victims. There is even a dog lying passively at the edge of the woods, looking in the opposite direction. In the far background, cattle are being driven along a road in the direction of a walled city. The whole painting seems to convey that violence was an accepted part of life during the Renaissance.

Such were manners and behavior in Europe at the dawn of modern times.

Name _____ Date _____

Think about Etiquette

You probably know that etiquette has to do with rules of behavior. Although Renaissance people were prone to acts of violence, they apparently worked hard at improving their conduct and manners.

How are your manners and social skills? How are those of your friends? Below are four situations that call for proper manners. Under each, write three applicable rules of conduct that every person who practices good etiquette should observe.

Dining

1. _____

2. _____

3. _____

Conversation

1. _____

2. _____

3. _____

In the Classroom

1. _____

2. _____

3. _____

In Public Places

1. _____

2. _____

3. _____

From *Everyday Life: The Renaissance* © 2005 GoodYear Books.

Name _____ Date _____

Complete a Checklist

To further test your knowledge of etiquette, put a check in front of what you consider the proper response to each of the situations presented below. Compare your responses with your classmates, and discuss them in class.

1. Young people should show respect to their elders
   _____ all the time.
   _____ only if their elders show respect in turn.
   _____ only when a situation calls for it.

2. While walking down the street with a girl, a boy should
   _____ walk on the side adjacent to stores and buildings.
   _____ walk on the side of the sidewalk next to the street.
   _____ walk on any side he chooses.

3. While out for a stroll with his wife, Mr. Manners bumps into a friend whom Mrs. Manners has never met. Mr. Manners should
   _____ not worry about introductions.
   _____ let his wife introduce herself.
   _____ introduce his wife to his friend.

4. Robert goes into a restaurant wearing his favorite baseball cap. Should he remove the cap?
   _____ It depends on the restaurant.
   _____ Yes, he should remove the cap.
   _____ It is completely up to Robert.

5. Megan's next-door neighbor, Mrs. Wilson, is 80 years old. Megan calls her by her first name. Is this proper etiquette?
   _____ No. Megan should refer to her as "Mrs. Wilson."
   _____ It really doesn't matter.
   _____ It is all right, if Mrs. Wilson doesn't object.

Name _____ Date _____

Point Out the Good and the Bad

Some people today might argue that our world, like that of Dickens's *A Tale of Two Cities,* exemplifies the best and the worst of times. With this in mind, write your thoughts on the lines provided under each statement.

It is the best of times because . . .

_____

_____

_____

_____

_____

_____

It is the worst of times because . . .

_____

_____

_____

_____

_____

I think the world would be a better place if . . .

_____

_____

_____

_____

_____

_____

From *Everyday Life: The Renaissance* © 2005 Good Year Books.

Name _____ Date _____

Write a Letter to the Editor

You are no doubt familiar with the editorial page of your newspaper. On this page, the editor or the publisher often gives his or her opinion on some important issue. Also, readers are given the opportunity to write letters expressing how they feel about issues, laws, and other matters that affect their lives daily. In addition, readers who disagree with any opinion expressed on the editorial page can write letters of rebuttal offering their personal views on a subject.

Pretend that newspapers existed during the Renaissance. Write a letter to the editor telling how you feel about the manners and/or behavior of the people of the times. Give three reasons why you feel as you do.

Dear Editor,

_____

_____

_____

_____

_____

_____

_____

_____

_____

_____

_____

_____

_____

_____

_____

_____

_____

_____

_____

_____

_____

(Your Name)

CHAPTER 8

Scientific Discoveries

While the people of the Renaissance were improving their manners and behavior, they took few steps to improve their knowledge of the universe and their physical world. Except for Leonardo da Vinci and others who learned much of anatomy by dissecting cadavers, little scientific progress was made until the latter part of the Renaissance period.

The Polish astronomer Copernicus, who discovered that the sun was the center of the universe.

Early Renaissance scientists continued to look to the ancient Greeks and Romans for guidance, accepting the errors those who lived long ago had made in their studies of both the world and the people who occupied it. Take their concept of the solar system, for example. Everyone accepted the geocentric theory put forth by the Greek scientist Ptolemy about A.D. 150. Ptolemy maintained that Earth was the center of the universe and that the sun and everything else revolved around it. After all, he erroneously pointed out, Earth did not move. And because it stood still, it must be the center of all creation.

People of the Middle Ages and the early years of the Renaissance cannot be faulted for believing Ptolemy. This was a time of religious fervor and, because God had placed people on Earth, then Earth had to be the center of the universe. So reasoned learned men of the times, even though a Greek scientist named Aristarchus had concluded some 300 years before Ptolemy that the sun was the center of the universe and all other bodies revolved around it. But Aristarchus's ideas were rejected, and humankind continued to be mired in ignorance for another 1,700 years.

The gap between medieval and Renaissance science was bridged by an English monk named Roger Bacon. Bacon, who lived in the 1200s, believed that knowledge could only be arrived at through observation and experimentation. His ideas, like those of Aristarchus centuries earlier, were also rejected. Bacon, in fact, spent more than 14 years of his life in prison for being so brazen as to challenge time-honored beliefs. Almost 200 years passed before his ideas were adopted and put into effect.

From *Everyday Life: The Renaissance* © 2005 GoodYear Books.

One of the first to emulate Bacon in his quest for scientific knowledge was a Polish astronomer named Nicolaus Copernicus. Copernicus was born in 1473 and was educated as a doctor and lawyer. He also was an ordained official of the Catholic Church. But his great love was astronomy, and he spent more than 30 years studying the heavens and formulating his theories.

Even as late as the 1500s, any scientific inquiry that contradicted the teachings of the Catholic Church resulted in punishment for the guilty party. Copernicus knew this and kept his thoughts to himself. To go against the established teachings of the Church made one a heretic and subject to scrutiny by the Inquisition, a special Church court that searched out and brought to trial any person who openly questioned Church doctrine. Torture (to extract confessions) and burnings at the stake were common punishments of this much-feared court.

In 1543, when he was almost 70 and had kept his ideas to himself for many years, Copernicus published *On the Revolutions of the Heavenly Spheres*. A copy was said to have been placed in his hands just before he died. In the book, Copernicus advanced the heliocentric theory that the sun—and not Earth—was the center of the universe. But because he did not have the wherewithal to test and prove his theory, his ideas were scoffed at and rejected. Both the educated and the uneducated laughed at the notion that Earth rotated on its axis. How silly, they thought! If Earth spun as Copernicus claimed, what kept people from simply flying off into space, never to be seen or heard from again?

Another century passed before Copernicus's theory could be proven. In the interval, the geocentric theory continued to be sanctioned by both the Church and leading scientists of the day. And woe to anyone who thought otherwise! There were always the rack, the thumbscrew, and the stake to convince any heretic of the error of his ways.

It was left to an Italian scientist named Galileo Galilei to prove that Copernicus was right. Galileo (1564–1642) had planned to become a doctor, but his interest in astronomy and mathematics got in the way. Through careful observation and study, he discovered both the principle of the pendulum and the law of falling bodies. You have probably studied in your science class how Galileo proved that if he dropped cannonballs of different weights from the top of the Leaning Tower of Pisa, they would touch the ground at about the same time.

Galileo, however, is remembered most for the telescope and for confirming the theories of Copernicus. Galileo didn't really invent the telescope; he made an improved model of one discovered by accident earlier by a Dutch optician named Johannes Lippershey. Lippershey was sometimes more interested in playing around with lenses than in making spectacles for his clients. In so doing, he found that he could arrange two lenses in such a way that he could make distant objects appear closer. Lippershey, however, viewed his spyglass as a toy with little practical use. It never occurred to him to aim his invention at the heavens.

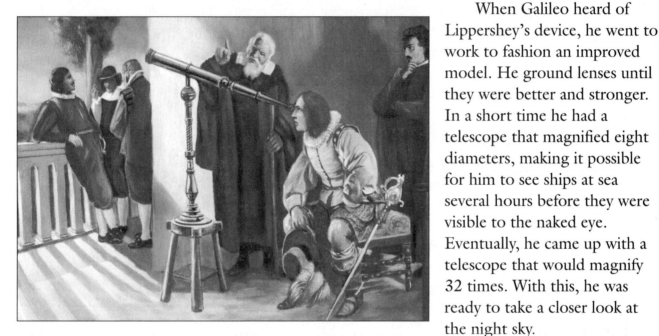

Nobles of Venice react with astonishment after gazing through Galileo's telescope.

When Galileo heard of Lippershey's device, he went to work to fashion an improved model. He ground lenses until they were better and stronger. In a short time he had a telescope that magnified eight diameters, making it possible for him to see ships at sea several hours before they were visible to the naked eye. Eventually, he came up with a telescope that would magnify 32 times. With this, he was ready to take a closer look at the night sky.

What Galileo saw when he first peered through his telescope was startling. The moon was not the smooth, flat body everyone supposed it to be. Instead, it was marked by valleys and craters. Galileo also marveled at the Milky Way and the rings of Saturn. His most remarkable discovery, however, concerned Jupiter. Through his telescope, Galileo could clearly see that the four moons of Jupiter revolved around that planet itself and not Earth. This was proof that all heavenly bodies did not circle Earth as was believed for centuries. Therefore, Galileo concluded that Earth could not be at the center of the universe.

Urban VIII, who became pope after Galileo proved Copernicus's heliocentric theory, authorized the astronomer to publish his findings. But there was a catch. He was ordered to present both his and Ptolemy's geocentric views as theories only. This, you will remember, was the official position held by the Church for centuries.

Galileo complied, and in 1632 he published his *Dialogue on the Two Chief World Systems.* But there was such an uproar over its contents that the bewildered author was arrested and brought before the dreaded Inquisition. Under threat of torture, he was forced to withdraw his theories and was placed under house arrest until his death in 1642.

In spite of continued opposition, Galileo's theories in time took root. They were supported by the work of a German mathematician and astronomer named Johannes Kepler (1571–1630), who had earlier explained the motion of the planets around the Sun. Kepler's calculations showed that the planets followed an oval path in their orbit, rather than a circular one as Copernicus had supposed. His laws of planetary motion proved essential to scientists in their study of the solar system.

As mentioned at the beginning of the chapter, few advancements in science were made during the Renaissance. Even the knowledge and theories advanced by Copernicus and Galileo did not occur until the later stages of the era. But there were several other achievements worthy of note. Johannes Gutenberg's printing press with movable type made it possible to print more books at a lower cost and, as a result, encouraged reading and education throughout Europe. Peter Henlein's "pocket" watch, although it was so heavy it had to be worn on a belt around the waist, relieved its carriers of the necessity of looking for a larger clock to learn the time. And Evangelista Torricelli's barometer in 1643 made it possible for the first time to measure air pressure, which is important in weather forecasting.

Although the Renaissance produced few scientific wonders, the groundwork for future discoveries had been laid. Roger Bacon's emphasis on experimentation and observation, coupled with the determination of such astronomers as Copernicus and Galileo, paved the way for the birth of modern science.

Johannes Kepler working at his desk. Kepler's calculations explained the laws of planetary motion.

Name _____ Date _____

Rank the Discoveries

In this chapter you studied several important achievements that stand out in an age not noted for its scientific progress. Which, in your opinion, was the most important? Which was the second in importance?

Rank these achievements 1 to 5 in the order of importance you assign them, with 1 being the most important and 5 being the least.

_____ Galileo's telescope

_____ Copernicus's heliocentric theory

_____ Gutenberg's printing press with movable type

_____ Roger Bacon's emphasis on observation and experimentation

_____ Leonardo da Vinci's anatomical discoveries

On the lines below, explain why you ranked the discoveries as you did.

_____

_____

_____

_____

_____

_____

_____

_____

_____

_____

_____

_____

_____

From *Everyday Life: The Renaissance* © 2005 Good Year Books.

Name _____   Date _____

Research the Solar System

You can imagine how astounded people were when Galileo and Kepler proved that the sun was center of the universe. Their work paved the way for the study of the solar system, which is made up of the sun and all the heavenly bodies that revolve around it.

Review the solar system in your science book or in an encyclopedia. Then answer the questions below.

1. List the names of the nine planets.

   _____   _____   _____

   _____   _____   _____

   _____   _____   _____

2. Which planet is nearest the sun? _____

3. Our solar system is part of a giant galaxy called

   _____

In the space below, make a drawing of the solar system showing all of the planets in the order of their distance from the sun. Color your drawing for effect.

Name _____ Date _____

Make False Statements True

All the statements at right are false. Change the word(s) in *italics* to make them true. Write the replacement word(s) on the line following the statement.

1. An astronomer named *Aristarchus* advanced the geocentric theory of the universe almost 2,000 years ago. _____

2. The geocentric theory holds that the *sun* is the center of the universe. _____

3. The Roman Catholic Church during the Middle Ages and the Renaissance upheld the *heliocentric* theory. _____

4. Roger Bacon believed that knowledge could only be arrived at by an *extensive study of the Bible*. _____

5. Nicolaus Copernicus was a *German* astronomer. _____

6. Copernicus published his theories about the universe in a book entitled *Dialogue on the Two Chief World Systems*. _____

7. A Dutch optician named *Peter Henlein* made the world's first crude telescope. _____

8. The telescope used by Galileo to study the heavens would magnify objects *eight* times. _____

9. The Inquisition was a special court established by the *rulers of the various Italian city-states*. _____

10. Johannes Kepler discovered that the planets followed a *circular* path in their movements around the sun. _____

11. Johannes Gutenberg is most remembered for inventing the *pocket watch*. _____

12. An Italian named Evangelista Torricelli devised an instrument to measure *temperature*. _____

From *Everyday Life: The Renaissance* © 2005 Good Year Books.

Name _____ Date _____

Create a Dialogue

You have learned that Galileo, like Copernicus before him, expounded the theory that the sun was the center of the universe. His support of the heliocentric theory brought him into conflict with the authorities of his day, who erroneously continued to maintain that Earth was the center of the universe and that all things revolved around it. By disregarding Ptolemy's geocentric theory, Galileo ran afoul of the Church and consequently spent the last 10 years of his life under house arrest.

Today you probably find it easy to support Galileo's theories in any discussion or debate. But how do you think you would fare if asked to defend the opposite view, that Galileo was a troublemaker and the geocentric theory was the correct explanation of the universe?

On the lines provided, create a dialogue between two Italian scientists of the 1600s as they point out reasons why Galileo's ideas are false.

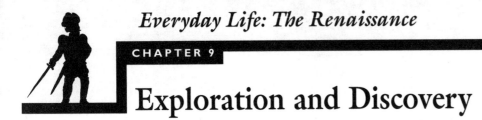

Exploration and Discovery

Water as thick as molasses, so that any ship that entered it would become stuck and rendered immobile? Certainly, thought people of the early Renaissance while discussing the seas beyond the equator.

Africans who had no heads but whose eyes and mouths were located in their chests? Yes, so believed some Europeans. After all, sailors who had ventured inland into Africa had seen such creatures with their very eyes! And what about those legless birds condemned to spend their entire lives in the air or men whose feet were so large that they could lay on their backs and use their feet as umbrellas? They were real too!

A terrible sea monster about to attack a ship. Sailors once believed that the oceans teemed with such creatures.

And huge, whirlpool-causing fish, who swam in circles around ships and sucked them to the bottom of the ocean? You better believe it! Or so went a popular tale that circulated at the time.

The people of the Middle Ages and the early Renaissance were as ignorant of the world as they were of the heavens. What they knew of geography consisted primarily of Europe and the lands surrounding the Mediterranean Sea. They did not know the true size of Africa and Asia and they had no knowledge whatever of the American continents. They were familiar with the Azores and Greenland islands in the North Atlantic Ocean, but that is where their geographical awareness ended.

You may be familiar with Europeans' belief in the Sea of Darkness, a term applied to the ocean beyond the known seas. It was a region of storms and fearsome monsters, where ships might enter but never exit. Huge sea serpents with massive jaws and powerful tails could break a ship in two in a second. Others that breathed fire could totally consume a vessel, killing all souls aboard. Still others could pluck screaming sailors from the decks of their ships and devour them in an instant. Even if a ship was fortunate enough to sail past all obstacles, it was sure to fall into oblivion, because it was generally held that Earth was flat. Or so it was believed by even learned people of the time.

From Everyday Life: The Renaissance © 2005 Good Year Books.

New navigational instruments slowly appeared that helped change Europeans' belief about the world and the oceans. One was the compass, an invention of both Europeans and the Chinese. The compass enabled mariners to tell in what direction they were traveling. Another was the astrolabe, which helped sailors calculate the position of the sun, moon, and stars and hence a ship's position at sea. Improved maps and better-built ships gave ship captains even more confidence as they ventured into previously unknown waters.

Beginning in the 1400s, what is commonly called "The Age of Exploration and Discovery" began. It stemmed from the desire of Europeans to find an all-water route to Asia, a route that would eliminate the need to ship goods from the East overland by caravan. Such a procedure was slow, dangerous, and costly. Along the way, caravans of traders were often attacked and robbed by bandits. They also had to pay rulers for the right to cross their lands, as well as dispense hefty fees to Italian sea captains for transporting the goods once they reached the Mediterranean. The prices charged for such goods upon reaching their destination were naturally high to offset the losses and expenses along the way.

The Portuguese took the lead in the Age of Exploration. This was due to the encouragement of Prince Henry, the son of King John I. Prince Henry believed that Asia could be reached by sailing around Africa. To this end, he established a school for navigators at Sagres on the Portuguese coast to study all aspects of sailing. Because of his interest in and support of exploration, Henry became known as "the Navigator."

The information assembled at Prince Henry's school led to several Portuguese expeditions along the west coast of Africa. One of the first was by Bartholomew Diaz (or Bartholomeu Dias) in 1486. With three ships he sailed the length of the African coast and rounded what came to be known as the Cape of Good Hope. He wanted to sail on to India, but his men threatened to mutiny if he did not turn back for Portugal. Eleven years later, in 1497, Vasco da Gama followed Diaz's route and sailed on to the port of Calicut, India. The goods he brought back to Portugal paid for the cost of the expedition some 60 times. More importantly, his voyage gave Portugal the first all-water route to the East and access to the riches of that region.

Even before the voyages of Diaz and da Gama, there was a sailor who believed the East could be reached by sailing west. His name was Christopher Columbus, and for years he tried to get some European ruler to finance such an expedition. Finally, in 1492, he received the backing of King Ferdinand and Queen Isabella of Spain. They gave him three ships—the *Nina,* the *Pinta,* and the *Santa Maria* —and sent him on his way.

Although Columbus was certainly right in maintaining that Earth was round, his estimate as to how far away Cipango (Japan) and Cathay (China) were from Europe was way off. Columbus reasoned that these countries were less than 3,000 miles out in the Ocean Sea, as the Atlantic was then known. He was wrong. Little did he realize that the Americas stood in the way and that Japan was more than 10,000 miles distant. He also had no way of knowing that some 70 days would pass before any land was sighted.

Columbus landing in the New World on the island of San Salvador.

You are familiar with the rest of the story. Columbus landed on San Salvador Island in the Bahamas on October 12, 1492. Thinking he had reached the East Indies, he called the natives who greeted him "Indians." (The region around where he landed later became known as the West Indies.) All told, Columbus made four trips to the "New World," thinking until his death that he had reached Asia. He never found the spices, gold, and jewels he sought, but his discoveries led to Spain claiming and settling most of the West Indies and Central and South America, as well as Mexico. Spanish colonies also were established in Florida, California, and the southwestern United States.

More Spanish expeditions followed in quick succession. In 1513, Vasco Nuñez de Balboa became the first European to reach the eastern shore of the Pacific Ocean. In 1519, Hernando Cortés conquered Mexico, and 14 years later, Francisco Pizarro overcame the Incas of Peru and added their realm to the Spanish Empire. In between, Ferdinand Magellan led an expedition that circumnavigated the globe, proving that the world was indeed round. Other Spanish conquistadors (conquerors) of note were Francisco Vasquez de Coronado and Hernando de Soto. Coronado explored the American southwest while looking for the mythical Seven Cities of Cibola. De Soto, also in search of gold, discovered the Mississippi River.

Three other European nations also financed voyages of exploration during the Renaissance. These were England, France, and the Netherlands. In the years following Columbus's discovery of the New World, attention focused on

From *Everyday Life: The Renaissance* © 2005 Good Year Books.

finding the "Northwest Passage." The Northwest Passage was believed to be a river or series of waterways leading through North America to Asia. It did not exist, but nations expended much time and money trying to find it.

In 1497, England sent John Cabot in search of the Northwest Passage. He failed to find it, but his exploration gave England claim to North America. Later, such French explorers as Jacques Cartier and Samuel de Champlain joined in the search. In spite of their failure, they made several important claims for the French crown. In 1534, Cartier discovered the St. Lawrence River, and, in 1609, Champlain was the first to gaze upon the Great Lakes. Because of their expeditions, and others that followed, France colonized Canada and the Great Lakes and Mississippi River regions.

The Netherlands got into the act in 1609. Henry Hudson, an Englishman in the service of the Dutch at the time, discovered the river in New York that came to bear his name. The following year, sailing for his native England, he discovered Hudson Bay in Canada. As a result of Hudson's explorations in the New York area, the Dutch founded the colony of New Netherland in 1624.

The Age of Exploration and Discovery is sometimes referred to as a "geographical Renaissance." Europeans gained knowledge of hitherto unknown regions of the world, establishing colonies and trading posts in India, Africa, and the East Indies, as well as in the Americas. They also gained easy access to spices and other goods that had previously been hard to come by. This period of broadening horizons is another reason why the Renaissance is looked upon as the beginning of modern times.

The Age of Exploration and Discovery is important to Americans for another reason. Had it not occurred and if the English had not established their 13 colonies along the Atlantic coast, the United States as we know it today might not have come into existence.

Sketch of a Spanish conquistador adorns a postage stamp.

Name _____ Date _____

Name That Notable

In the box are the names of famous explorers and others who played a major role in the Age of Exploration and Discovery. Write the name of the correct person(s) on the blank line in front of each statement.

Balboa

Cabot

Cartier

Champlain

Columbus

Coronado

Cortés

da Gama

De Soto

Diaz

Ferdinand and Isabella

Hudson

Magellan

Pizarro

Prince Henry

1. _____ "I conquered the Incas of Peru."

2. _____ "My explorations led to the Dutch establishing the colony of New Netherland."

3. _____ "I was the first European to see the eastern shore of the Pacific Ocean."

4. _____ "I conquered Mexico for Spain."

5. _____ "I was the first to see the Great Lakes."

6. _____ "I died never knowing I had discovered the New World."

7. _____ "I led the first expedition to sail around the world."

8. _____ "England's claim to North America was based on my expedition in 1497."

9. _____ "I discovered the St. Lawrence River."

10. _____ "I established a school for navigators in Portugal."

11. _____ "I searched for the Seven Cities of Cibola."

12. _____ "We gave Columbus ships to sail to the New World."

13. _____ "I was the first to sail to the tip of Africa."

14. _____ "I discovered the Mississippi River."

15. _____ "I sailed around the Cape of Good Hope to India in 1497."

From Everyday Life: The Renaissance © 2005 GoodYear Books.

Name _____ Date _____

Make a Cereal-Box Report

There are many more explorers who had an impact on the geographical Renaissance than the ones you read about in this chapter. From the information presented in the chapter, prepare a cereal-box report on one notable person referred to in chapter 9. You may find additional facts about that person in any encyclopedia. What you will need and how to proceed are listed opposite.

Here Are the Things You Will Need:

1. An empty cereal box, or any similar box

2. White paper, such as typing or printer paper

3. Glue or paste

4. A felt-tipped pen, or any pen suitable for drawing

5. Scissors

Here Is What You Do:

1. Glue or paste white paper over all the sides of the cereal box.

2. On the top edge of the box, write the name of the person you have researched, along with your name in small print.

3. On one side panel, write the name of the country the person represented.

4. On the other side panel, write a sentence describing what that person accomplished.

5. On the front of the box, draw a rough sketch of the person on whom you are reporting.

6. On the back of the box, list several facts about the person that were not listed in the narrative of this chapter.

Name _____ Date _____

Use Your Critical-Thinking Skills

Write your best answers to the questions posed opposite.

1. How do you think superstitions and rumors about the dangers of sailing far out into the oceans got started?

_____
_____
_____
_____

2. Why do you think Columbus had such great difficulty in obtaining financial backing for his expedition?

_____
_____
_____
_____

3. Suppose that European explorers had never "discovered" the New World. In what ways do you think the history of the Americas might have been different?

_____
_____
_____
_____

4. What similarities exist between today's space explorations and the expeditions of European explorers 500 years ago?

_____
_____
_____
_____

From *Everyday Life: The Renaissance* © 2005 Good Year Books.

Name _____   Date _____

Solve Some Exploration Math

Solve the four word problems here and write the answers on the appropriate lines. Space is provided to work each problem.

1. Christopher Columbus thought Japan was about 2,500 miles from Europe. Remembering that 1 mile equals 0.62 kilometers, how many kilometers away did Columbus assume Japan to be? Round your answer.

    _____ kilometers

2. We know today that Japan is really some 16,000 kilometers from Europe. In round numbers, how many miles is this equal to?

    _____ miles

3. Seventy days passed before Columbus sighted land on October 12, 1492. By that date, he had sailed some 3,000 miles. How many miles, in round numbers, did his ships average each day?

    _____ miles

4. The speed of ships is measured in knots rather than in miles per hour. For the sake of simplicity, however, compute how many miles per hour Columbus's ships attained as they made their way across the Atlantic.

    _____ mph

Great Religious Changes

At the same time that the Age of Exploration was in full swing, another event was beginning that would have a profound effect on people everywhere. That event was the Protestant Revolt, a period in the 1500s when various Protestant denominations came into existence. (The Protestant Revolt is referred to in some history texts as the Protestant Reformation. That is in some ways a misnomer. It was the Protestants who protested or revolted; it was the Roman Catholic Church that reformed itself as a result of this revolt.)

Martin Luther posting his *95 Theses* on the door of his church at Wittenberg, Germany. What was his purpose in doing so?

You are no doubt familiar with the phrase "to stir up a hornet's nest." Whether one chooses to call them hornets, wasps, or yellow jackets, to stir them up invites the "stirrer" a whole lot of trouble! One person who "stirred up a hornet's nest" with regard to the Roman Catholic Church was Martin Luther.

Martin Luther was a priest in the German town of Wittenberg. He had not planned to come into conflict with his church. In fact, he had not even planned to become a priest. Although always devout and preoccupied with the issues of death and salvation, Luther originally studied to enter the legal profession. But an incident that occurred on July 2, 1505, changed his future profession and his life forever. Returning from a visit to his parents' home in the town of Mansfield, he was overtaken by a severe thunderstorm. Suddenly a bolt of lightning struck a nearby tree, and the electrical discharge threw him to the ground. Taking this as a sign, Luther, by his own account, cried, "Help, St. Anna, I will become a monk!" And he did, much to the sorrow of his father Hans, who had worked hard to see his son through law school.

In 1505, at the age of 22, Luther entered the monastery at Erfurt. Two years later he was ordained a priest, and five years later he became a professor of theology at the University of Wittenberg. He also preached on occasion at one of the city's churches. Had he not become embroiled in a bitter dispute with the Church, he might have lived out his life as a well-liked and respected teacher of religion.

From *Everyday Life: The Renaissance* © 2005 Good Year Books.

But that was not to be. In 1510, Luther was sent on a special mission to Rome. Although he was enthralled with the ancient city and enjoyed taking in the sights, he was shocked by the manners and behavior of the people, the clergy included. He returned home deeply troubled by what he had seen.

Other practices of the Roman Catholic Church also bothered Luther. The most important of these was the sale of indulgences. An indulgence was a partial forgiveness for sins. But the Church still required that a person granted an indulgence go on a pilgrimage or perform some other good works to atone for sins. But indulgences were never sold until the Church began to raise money to finance the building of St. Peter's Church in Rome. Representatives of the Church traveled throughout Europe selling indulgences as a way to raise money. Poor, illiterate people misunderstood the idea of indulgences and believed that a mere payment of money would buy forgiveness of their sins and ensure salvation. Representatives of the Church did nothing to educate the people about indulgences and took their money eagerly.

Luther felt that the selling of indulgences was wrong and that it violated the principles of the Church. Always one to welcome debate, he posted what became known as the *95 Theses* on the door of All Saints' Church in Wittenberg in 1517. As mentioned earlier, he had no thought of breaking with the Church. His only purpose was to discuss with interested persons things he considered wrong with the Church and seek ways to bring about reforms. One thing, however, led to another, and Luther soon found himself in trouble with the pope.

In addition to condemning the sale of indulgences, Luther also attacked traditional Church doctrine. He began to preach that salvation did not result from good works but was instead based on faith, and faith alone. According to Luther, all the good works a person performed and all the money he or she gave to the Church was of no avail. Only true faith guaranteed one a ticket to heaven. Luther also rejected all the sacraments, or holy rites of the Church, except baptism and communion.

Now Luther had gone too far. In 1520, Pope Leo X had had enough of his heresy and sent him a letter ordering him to mend his ways or face excommunication. Luther responded by burning the pope's letter in public. The following year, the rebellious priest was ordered to appear before the Diet (assembly) of Worms (pronounced "varms"), a special council that convened in a town of that name. Again, Luther was ordered to take back the things he had said. When he refused, he was declared a heretic and an outlaw. This meant

From Everyday Life: The Renaissance © 2005 Good Year Books.

that anyone could kill him without fear of reprisal. Luther would have certainly met a violent end had he not been granted refuge in the castle of a friendly German prince.

Luther spent a year in hiding, during which time he translated the Bible into German. By this time, his ideas had spread and become popular in other regions of Germany. Many German princes supported Luther because they envied the vast wealth of the Roman Catholic Church and the lands it controlled. When Luther's doctrines continued to be officially banned by the Church, these princes protested, giving rise to the term *Protestant*. Afterward, any church that was not Roman Catholic or Eastern Orthodox was referred to as Protestant.

John Calvin, who established a strict kind of Protestantism in Switzerland.

Luther's beliefs led to the establishment of the Lutheran Church. Again, its doctrine emphasized faith over good works and the sacraments. Lutheranism spread throughout northern Germany and into the Scandinavian countries. By the end of the 1500s, nearly all of Scandinavia had become Lutheran.

Other Protestant movements followed. In Switzerland, John Calvin established a strict form of Protestantism that became the basis of various denominations throughout Europe. Presbyterians in Scotland, Huguenots in France, and Puritans in England all based their doctrines on the teachings of Calvin, who denounced such practices as dancing, card playing, and showy dress. The Congregational Church established by the Puritans in Massachusetts in the early 1600s was founded on Calvin's principles.

The Protestant Revolt in England took a different turn than that on the Continent. Although the ideas of Luther and Calvin took some root there, the conflict between the English and the Roman Catholic Church was more political than religious. In short, it was a conflict between King Henry VIII and papal authorities in Rome.

Henry VIII was a headstrong ruler and a devout Catholic who had persecuted early Protestants in his country. But Henry had a problem. His wife, Catherine, the daughter of Ferdinand and Isabella of Spain, had not given birth to a son to carry on the family name. So in 1527, Henry asked Pope Clement VII to annul (cancel) his marriage to Catherine so he could wed a lady of the court named Anne Boleyn. When the pope refused, Henry broke with the Catholic Church and set up the Church of England.

From *Everyday Life: The Renaissance* © 2005 Good Year Books.

The various Protestant churches and denominations that sprang up in the 1500s differed from the Roman Catholic Church in a number of ways. First, and foremost, they were organized and governed on a national rather than a universal level. Second, some permitted the clergy to marry. (Martin Luther himself married and fathered six children.) Third, services were held in the everyday language of the people and not in Latin. Fourth, supreme authority rested with the scriptures and not the head of the church.

As a result of the Protestant Revolt, the Roman Catholic Church took steps to correct the abuses that had brought on Luther's rebellion in 1517. More able and sincere men were selected as popes and the training and morals of priests and monks were addressed and improved. Simony, the buying and selling of church offices, and nepotism, the placing of friends and relatives in important positions, were outlawed, as was the sale of indulgences. These steps were taken by the Council of Trent, a Church Council that met between 1545 and 1563 in Trent, Italy.

The movement on the part of the Roman Catholic Church to check the effects of the Protestant Revolt is referred to as the Counter Reformation. It also included the efforts of the Society of Jesus, or Jesuits, a religious order founded by Ignatius Loyola. The Jesuits were successful in restoring some parts of eastern Europe to Catholicism. In addition, the Inquisition, the special Church court established to bring heretics to trial, saw to it that anyone supporting Protestant ideas in such Catholic nations as Italy and Spain was quickly silenced.

The Protestant Revolt did more than bring about new religious denominations and weaken the power of the Roman Catholic Church. It greatly increased the power of rulers and further enhanced the growth of strong national states. However, bloody massacres and religious wars characterized much of Europe for some time afterward.

King Henry VIII, who broke with the Roman Catholic Church and started the Church of England in 1527.

Name _____ Date _____

Conduct an Interview

Suppose that newspapers existed in the 1500s and that you are a reporter for the *Wittenberg Weekly*. Your editor, upon hearing that Martin Luther has just burned the letter from the pope ordering him to stop his attack on the Church, immediately dispatches you to interview the disobedient priest.

What questions would you ask Luther? What answers do you think he would give? Write your imagined interview on the lines below.

_____

_____

_____

_____

_____

_____

_____

_____

_____

_____

_____

_____

_____

_____

_____

_____

_____

_____

_____

_____

_____

_____

_____

_____

From Everyday Life: The Renaissance © 2005 Good Year Books.

Name _____ Date _____

Solve a Protestant Revolt Puzzle

ACROSS

2 Putting friends and relatives in office

5 What Luther translated into German

7 John _____, Protestant leader in Switzerland

9 Special Church court

10 Luther's 95 _____

12 Luther's father

13 _____ of Worms

DOWN

1 Founder of the Jesuits

3 Home of the Huguenots

4 English Calvinists

6 A pardon for sin

7 Henry VIII's first wife

8 What Luther stressed over good works

11 Buying and selling of Church offices

Name _____ Date _____

Organize Organized Religion

Even before the Protestant Revolt began in 1517, the Christian Church had split into two major divisions: the Roman Catholic Church and the Eastern Orthodox Church. The Protestant Revolt added a third division.

While most of Europe and the colonies that sprang up in the New World all followed the Christian faith, rival religions had existed for centuries in other regions of the world. With these facts in mind, consult an encyclopedia or other source and answer these questions.

1. List any 5 of the world's major religions and their principle locations.

Religion	Where Located
1. _____	_____
2. _____	_____
3. _____	_____
4. _____	_____
5. _____	_____

2. There are more than 20 Protestant denominations in existence today. List any 10.

1. _____
2. _____
3. _____
4. _____
5. _____
6. _____
7. _____
8. _____
9. _____
10. _____

From *Everyday Life: The Renaissance* © 2005 Good Year Books.

Name _____ *Date* _____

Complete a Chain of Events Staircase

Complete the staircase below by filling in Events 2–5 in the story of Martin Luther's break with the Roman Catholic Church. Don't be concerned if your sequence of events differs from those of your class-mates. The idea is to place significant events in the order in which they occurred.

Event 1, Luther's posting of his *95 Theses*, has been done for you. Fill in what you consider to be the next four events that occurred between Luther's initial act of rebellion and the establishment of the Lutheran Church.

Event 5
_____

Event 4
_____

Event 3
_____

Event 2
_____

Event 1
Luther posts 95 Theses.

CHAPTER 11

The Renaissance Spreads

Many books on the Renaissance deal primarily with Italy. They focus on the contributions of such great artists as Michelangelo and Leonardo da Vinci, on the writings of the renowned humanist Petrarch and others, and on the works of famous sculptors such as Lorenzo Ghiberti. But the Renaissance spread elsewhere in Europe. France, England, the Netherlands, the German states, and Spain all experienced a renewed interest in learning and the arts. The main difference was that the Renaissance began in these countries much later and extended into the 1600s.

The Dutch scholar Desiderius Erasmus. In his book *The Praise of Folly*, he criticized the Roman Catholic Church.

In chapter 2 you read about the Dutch priest Desiderius Erasmus. At that time, you learned that he was one of the most influential figures of the northern Renaissance. Although he did not support the Protestant movement, he was very critical of the Roman Catholic Church and attacked it in his book *The Praise of Folly*.

Are you familiar with the term *satire*? A satire is a story, poem, or essay that ridicules or attacks a custom or an institution. It makes use of wit and sarcasm in poking fun at the object of its criticism. In *The Praise of Folly*, Erasmus directed his satire toward the Roman Catholic Church, as well as to human weaknesses that were so glaring at the time.

At no point did Erasmus attack the teachings of the Church. His concern centered around the ignorance and the behavior of many of the clergy. He ridiculed such things as greed, gluttony, arrogance, and intolerance. He also scolded some clergy for having taken wives and mistresses, something they were forbidden to do by the laws of the Church. Besides promoting religious reforms, Erasmus encouraged people to use reason in making decisions. His influence led to a study of the ancient classics in northern Europe.

New ideas were more easily spread throughout northern and western Europe because of Johannes Gutenberg's printing press. (You will remember that he was mentioned briefly in chapter 8.) Gutenberg's press replaced methods that had been introduced by the Chinese. About A.D. 600 the Chinese invented block printing. With block printing, images are carved on wooden blocks, dipped in ink, and pressed onto paper. Some 500 years later, the Chinese

From *Everyday Life: The Renaissance* © 2005 Good Year Books.

began to use movable clay letters that could be used over again. Gutenberg's press used metal type, setting into motion the age of modern printing.

You have already learned that Gutenberg's press made possible the printing of more books—and at a much lower cost. Within 50 years of its invention, more than 30,000 different books were in circulation throughout Europe. The printing press also resulted in greater accuracy and uniformity in printed material. More importantly, it encouraged education and led to the rise of a more informed public. The latter was instrumental in forming the basis of democratic governments that appeared later.

The printing press with movable type also helped spur the development of national literatures. Whereas books had previously been handwritten in Latin and Greek, they now began to appear printed in the vernacular, the everyday language of the people. French writers wrote in French and English writers wrote in English, for example. Whether in France, England, Spain, or elsewhere, people could purchase books written in a language they could understand. The result was, as mentioned above, a better-educated and a more informed citizenry.

It is not the purpose of this chapter to discuss the lives and works of the many northern European authors who wrote during the late Renaissance. But one writer of this period stands head and shoulders above the rest and deserves our attention. That writer was William Shakespeare.

Johannes Gutenberg demonstrating his printing press with movable type.

William Shakespeare was an actor as well as a playwright. He was also a poet and is known to have written some 154 sonnets, which are poems of 14 lines. But it is as a playwright that Shakespeare is best known. Some sources credit him with more than 30 plays. These plays are divided into three groups: tragedies, histories, and comedies. A tragedy is a story with an unhappy or disastrous ending. In a tragedy the main character is unsuccessful in what he or she is trying to do. You are probably familiar with Romeo and Juliet, one of Shakespeare's most popular tragedies. It is a tragedy because the lovers Romeo and Juliet are frustrated in their goal of being together and end up dead at the conclusion of the play.

From Everyday Life: The Renaissance © 2005 Good Year Books.

An explanation of a history is not necessary, but a description of a comedy is in order. Contrary to what many people believe, a comedy is not necessarily a rib-tickling affair in which the audience rolls in the aisles with laughter. What makes a comedy different from a tragedy is that it has a happy ending. What some people call a comedy is really a farce, a production characterized by ridiculous lines and absurd happenings. A popular Shakespeare comedy with which you might be familiar is *The Taming of the Shrew.* As used in the title, the word *shrew* refers to a bad-tempered, quarrelsome woman. In the play, a determined husband, Petruchio, successfully "tames" Katharina, his cross and scolding wife.

A sketch of the original Globe Theater. The theater opened in 1599.

Shakespeare was a member of an acting company called the Chamberlain's Men. In 1599, this group, led by actors Richard and Cuthbert Burbage, built the Globe Theater in London. It was here that most of Shakespeare's plays were first performed. The original Globe stood for only 14 years, for in 1613 a cannon fired during a play set the roof on fire and the building was totally destroyed. It was rebuilt the following year, only to be destroyed again in 1644. This time the destruction was on purpose. The Puritan government that controlled England at the time frowned on the theater and had the Globe torn down. Today a replica of the Globe stands on the same side of the Thames River in London where the old Globe once stood. Shakespeare's plays are performed in the open air, as they were in his time.

The Globe's stage jutted out into the audience. There were covered seats for viewers who could afford to pay. Those who could not were permitted to stand in the open and watch for a penny. Members of all classes attended, from housewives to visitors from abroad. Plays always started at 2 in the afternoon so children could also attend.

From *Everyday Life: The Renaissance* © 2005 Good Year Books.

Space does not permit mention of all the writers and artists who contributed to the Renaissance in the north and other parts of Europe. While Shakespeare was one of the most important, there were many others. Most were encouraged and funded by either monarchs or wealthy patrons. They included the artists Albrecht Dürer, Pieter Breughel, and El Greco and such renowned writers as François Rabelais, Miquel Cervantes, and Sir Thomas More. Almost every western European country could boast of a number of talented individuals.

Some cities stood out in their support of the arts. One was the German city of Nuremberg. Because it was home to one of Europe's first printing presses, the city had a library that contained some 4,000 volumes. Artists, scholars, printers, mapmakers, and others flocked to Nuremberg.

So there you have it: a 300-year period in European history referred to as the Renaissance. Why, again, was this age so important? The reasons are many. Europeans broke from the medieval practice of thinking only of the hereafter and began to concentrate on life in this world. They began to think in what later came to be known as modern terms. They sailed the oceans and discovered new lands, peoples, and products. They developed an appreciation for the arts and a real interest in learning. They established new religious faiths and eliminated the abuses within the one church that had existed for centuries. Finally, they formed national governments that helped end feudalism in most places.

One of the most important results of the Renaissance was that it promoted the dignity and worth of the individual. Previously, people were secondary to everything going on in the world. A person's main goal was to prepare for heaven; little else mattered. The Renaissance changed this concept, creating a new outlook on life that would in time have a tremendous impact on the social and political affairs of Europe.

Name _____ Date _____

Write Your Opinions

Tell why you agree or disagree with each of the statements below.

1. The printing press is the greatest invention in the history of humankind.

   _____

   _____

   _____

2. William Shakespeare was by far the most outstanding personage of the entire Renaissance period.

   _____

   _____

   _____

3. Other parts of Europe contributed more to the fine arts than Renaissance Italy.

   _____

   _____

   _____

4. The Protestant Revolt was the best thing that ever happened to the Roman Catholic Church.

   _____

   _____

   _____

5. The most important result of the Renaissance was that people stopped taking religion so seriously.

   _____

   _____

   _____

From *Everyday Life: The Renaissance* © 2005 Good Year Books.

Name _____ Date _____

Make a Drawing of the Globe Theater

In the space provided, make a sketch of the Globe Theater where many of Shakespeare's plays were first performed. You can find samples on the Internet, in encyclopedias, or in books dealing with either Shakespeare or the Renaissance.

On the lines at the bottom of the page, write a brief description of the Globe Theater as it appeared in Shakespeare's time.

_____

_____

_____

_____

_____

_____

Name _____ Date _____

Distinguish between Sentences and Fragments

Can you distinguish between a complete sentence and a fragment? Fragments are statements that either lack a verb or a subject or do not express a complete thought. Fragments may be used in certain situations, but it is usually best to use complete sentences when writing.

At the right is a group of statements relating to chapter 11. Some are fragments, while others are complete sentences. On the line at the end of each, write F if the statement is a fragment or S if it is a sentence. In the space below each statement that you mark as a fragment, rewrite the statement to make it a complete sentence.

1. The Renaissance in northern Europe. _____

    _____

2. *The Praise of Folly* is a satire written by Desiderius Erasmus. _____

    _____

3. After Johannes Gutenberg invented the printing press with movable type. _____

    _____

    _____

4. William Shakespeare, possibly the greatest writer of all time. _____

    _____

5. Renaissance writers wrote in the everyday language of the people. _____

    _____

6. The original Globe Theater burned to the ground in 1613. _____

    _____

7. While Shakespeare was turning out plays in England, playwrights in other countries were doing the same. _____

    _____

    _____

8. Because Nuremberg supported the fine arts. _____

    _____

From Everyday Life: The Renaissance © 2005 Good Year Books.

Name _____ Date _____

Write a Summary

On the lines provided, write a summary of the causes, events, and results of the Renaissance. Be sure to use your best grammar and sentence structure as you describe this significant period of history.

_____
_____
_____
_____
_____
_____
_____
_____
_____
_____
_____
_____
_____
_____
_____
_____
_____
_____
_____
_____
_____
_____
_____
_____
_____
_____

Answers to Activities

Chapter 1
Distinguish between Fact and Opinion
1. F 2. F 3. O 4. F 5. O 6. F 7. O 8. O 9. F
10. O 11. O 12. F 13. F 14. O

Make False Statements True
1. Dark Ages 2. Vikings 3. German king 4. weak
5. recapture the Holy Land from the Muslim Turks
6. longbow 7. monk 8. Chinese 9. cannon
10. English 11. coming into contact with flea-
infested rats 12. one-third 13. Italy
14. Mediterranean

Use Your Critical-Thinking Skills
Answers should be similar to the following:
1. Little progress was made, and art and learning almost ceased.
2. A serf was considered part of the land and was sold along with it. Slaves were bought and sold separately.
3. Contact with the advanced civilizations of the East helped end feudalism and spur trade, as well as bring about the growth of towns and universities.
4. No one understood what caused it or how to prevent it.
5. Because people's interest turned to things other than just religion

Chapter 2
Solve a Humanism Puzzle
1. Father 2. Laura 3. Romans 4. Petrarch
5. Manuscripts 6. Religion 7. Perspective
8. Erasmus

Point Out the Differences
Answers should be similar to the following:
1. Life: Medieval people saw life as simply a preparation for the hereafter. Renaissance people thought life was to be enjoyed to the fullest.
2. Art: Medieval art was lifeless and focused on religion. Subjects were stiff and had little form. Renaissance art emphasized reality through the use of color, shadow, and perspective.

3. Religion: Religion dominated medieval life. People were considered sinners who could only look to the hereafter for a better life. Renaissance people did not forsake religion, but they believed they could be religious and enjoy life at the same time.

Name Those Synonyms and Antonyms
Answers will vary, but the following synonyms and antonyms are common.
1. tolerant; prejudice 2. reputation; anonymity
3. recent; old-fashioned 4. useless; valuable 5. quit;
retained 6. commend; condemn 7. condemning;
praiseworthy 8. fortunate; failing 9. came; left
10. zeal; indifference 11. unreal; actual 12. inspiring;
discouraging 13. favorite; unpopular 14. proceeds;
stops 15. praised; disapproved 16. revering;
disliking 17. stiff; relaxed 18. current; former
19. unfamiliarity; knowledge 20. like; abhor

Chapter 3
Solve Some Sistine Chapel Math
1a. 5,940 1b. 552 2. 279 3. 2,152

Use Context Clues to Complete Sentences
produced; greater; excelled; primarily;
contributions; accomplished; drew; modern;
models; study; statues; unsurpassed; attest; second;
construction; agree

Chapter 4
Use Your Critical-Thinking Skills
Answers will vary.

Fill in a Venn Diagram
Answers will vary but should be similar to the following:
Renaissance Marriages: Marriages were arranged; girls were betrothed at a very young age; marriage had nothing to do with love; girls had to have a dowry.
Both: Huge sums were often spent on weddings; a wife and children were looked upon as blessings; families were usually close-knit and loving.

From Everyday Life: The Renaissance © 2005 GoodYear Books.

Modern Marriages: Are not arranged in most countries, and no dowry is required; most places require the bride and groom to be a certain age; child brides are generally forbidden.

Solve Some Wedding-Related Math

1. 1,421   2. 203   3. 182   4. 327   5. 165

Complete a Word Search

E	X	Z	E	R	**V**	K	L	P	**M**	**C**	V	W	**S**	O
X	Y	**W**	**E**	**D**	**D**	**I**	**N**	**G**	B	A	K	L	**O**	T
T	M	**C**	**R**	**O**	**Y**	**A**	**L**	C	D	**N**	**N**	F	**C**	T
R	G	O	H	**W**	C	A	T	L	Q	**T**	R	**T**	**I**	U
A	E	U	G	R	S	T	U	V	**A**	**A**	B	B	**E**	H
V	**I**	**N**	**E**	**Y**	**A**	**R**	**D**	K	**P**	T	L	L	**T**	L
A	B	**T**	A	C	D	H	**P**	S	**P**	**A**	U	U	**Y**	V
G	E	**E**	F	I	**J**	O	**E**	K	**R**	L	L	**M**	**B**	G
A	B	**S**	C	D	**S**	**U**	A	F	**E**	F	H	**A**	**A**	Z
N	O	**S**	M	N	**T**	**S**	**S**	T	N	V	V	**R**	**C**	D
C	H	A	I	R	**I**	**E**	A	Z	T	K	Z	**R**	**H**	E
E	T	R	A	L	**G**	**H**	**N**	**N**	I	K	K	**I**	**E**	C
S	T	O	R	M	**M**	**O**	**T**	T	C	K	G	**A**	**L**	Z
S	U	E		**I**	**T**	**A**	**L**	**Y**	B	E	**E**	T	**G**	**O**	T
D	A	D	D	Y	Z	**D**	**W**	**I**	**D**	**O**	**W**	**E**	**R**	K

Chapter 5

Match Foods and Countries

1. C   2. A   3. C   4. B   5. D   6. F   7. D   8. B
9. A   10. E   11. G   12. G   13. D   14. J   15. G
16. D   17. H   18. H   19. I   20. I

Solve a Fashion and Food Puzzle

Across: 1. corset   5. doublet   9. farthingale
   12. beer   13. fork   14. wool   15. Venus
Down: 2. tomato   3. ruff   4. blonde   6. butterfly
   7. water   8. wine   10. Arabic   11. turkey

Chapter 6

Interpret a Pie Graph

1. 6   2. 42   3. 18   4. 36   5. 18

Indicate Which Word Does Not Belong

1. helmets. Helmets are not associated with hunting.
2. serf. A serf is not one of the pieces used in chess.
3. lute. A lute was not part of a knight's outfit.
4. ball. A ball has nothing to do with bullfighting.
5. dominoes. Dominoes are not associated with gambling.
6. fireworks. Fireworks are not part of a parade.
7. advisor. An advisor is not an entertainer.
8. All Saints Day. All Saints Day is not a pre-Lent carnival.
9. tennis. Tennis is a sport played by individuals.
10. Florida. Florida is a state, not a city.

Chapter 7

Think about Etiquette

Answers will vary.

Complete a Checklist

1. all the time   2. walk on the side of the sidewalk next to the street   3. introduce his wife to his friend   4. Yes, he should remove his cap.
5. No. Megan should refer to her as "Mrs. Wilson."

Point Out the Good and the Bad

Answers will vary.

Chapter 8

Rank the Discoveries

Answers will vary.

Research the Solar System

1. Mercury, Mars, Uranus, Venus, Jupiter, Neptune, Earth, Saturn, Pluto
2. Mercury
3. The Milky Way

Make False Statements True

1. Ptolemy   2. Earth   3. geocentric
4. through observation and experimentation
5. Polish   6. On the Revolutions of the Heavenly Spheres   7. Johannes Lippershey   8. 32
9. Roman Catholic Church   10. oval
11. printing press   12. air pressure

Chapter 9

Name That Notable

1. Pizarro   2. Hudson   3. Balboa   4. Cortés
5. Champlain   6. Columbus   7. Magellan   8. Cabot
9. Cartier   10. Prince Henry   11. Coronado
12. Ferdinand and Isabella   13. Diaz   14. De Soto
15. da Gama

Use Your Critical-Thinking Skills

Answers will vary but should be similar to the following:

1. unexplained disappearances of ships; sightings of whales, manatees, and other strange creatures of the sea
2. No one believed the East could be reached by sailing west. Many people still believed Earth was flat.
3. Answers will vary considerably.
4. excitement; thrill of adventure; possible fear of the unknown

Solve Some Exploration Math

1. 4,000   2. 10,000   3. 43   4. 1.8

Chapter 10

Solve a Protestant Revolt Puzzle

Across: 2. nepotism   5. Bible   7. Calvin
    9. Inquisition   10. Theses   12. Hans   13. Diet
Down: 1. Loyola   3. France   4. Puritans
    6. indulgence   7. Catherine   8. faith
    11. simony

Organize Organized Religion

1. The five principal religions are: Christianity (Europe, North and South America); Judaism (Israel, United States, Russia); Islam (Middle East, Africa, Indonesia); Hinduism (India); Buddhism (China, Japan, Tibet, southeastern Asia)

Students might also list Shinto (Japan) and Confucianism and Taoism (China).

2. Students might list any of the following: Methodist, Baptist, Presbyterian, Church of God, Church of Christ, Church of England, Adventist, Quakers, Jehovah's Witnesses, Latter-Day Saints, Mennonite, Pentecostal, Reformed, Church of the Nazarene, Anglican, Christian Scientists, Brethren, Unitarian, African Methodist Episcopal, Episcopal.

Complete a Chain of Events Staircase

Answers will vary but might include the following steps: Luther's burning of the pope's letter; Luther's appearance before the Diet of Worms; Luther finding refuge in the castle of a friendly prince; Luther translating the Bible into German.

Chapter 11

Write Your Opinions

Answers will vary.

Distinguish between Sentences and Fragments

1. F   2. S   3. F   4. F   5. S   6. S   7. S   8. F
Students' sentences will vary.

Additional Resources

Books for Children

Cairns, Trevor. *The Birth of Modern Europe*. Minneapolis: Lerner Publications Company, 1975.

Caselli, Giovanni. *The Renaissance and the New World*. New York: Peter Bedrick Books, 1985.

Langley, Andrew. *Renaissance*. New York: Alfred A. Knopf, 1999.

Books for Adults

Bortolon, Liana. *The Life, Times, and Art of Leonardo*. New York: Crescent Books, 1965.

Durant, Will. *The Renaissance*. New York: Simon and Schuster, 1953.

Hale, John. *The Civilization of Europe in the Renaissance*. New York: Antheneum, 1994.

Rabb, Theodore K. *Renaissance Lives: Portraits of an Age*. New York: Pantheon Books, 1993.

Rizzitti, Maria Luisa. *The Life, Times and Art of Michelangelo*. New York: Crescent Books, 1966.